COSPLAY BASICS
A BEGINNERS GUIDE TO THE ART OF COSTUME PLAY

ONE PEACE BOOKS

Cosplay Basics: A Beginners Guide to the Art of Costume Play

Original Japanese Edition

Hajimetedemo Anshin Kosupure Nyuumon by Yuki Takasou, RUMINE and

TREND-PRO

© 2011 by Takasou, RUMINE and TREND-PRO Published by Ohmsha, Ltd.

English Translation published by One Peace Books by arrangement with Ohmsha, Ltd. through

Japan UNI Agency, Inc. © 2015.

ISBN 978-1-935548-81-2

Text by Yuki Takasou & RUMINE

Illustrations by Kashiko Kurobuchi

Production by TREND-PRO

English Edition Published by One Peace Books 2015

Printed in Canada

2nd printing May 2015

One Peace Books

43-32 22nd Street STE 204 Long Island City New York 11101

www.onepeacebooks.com

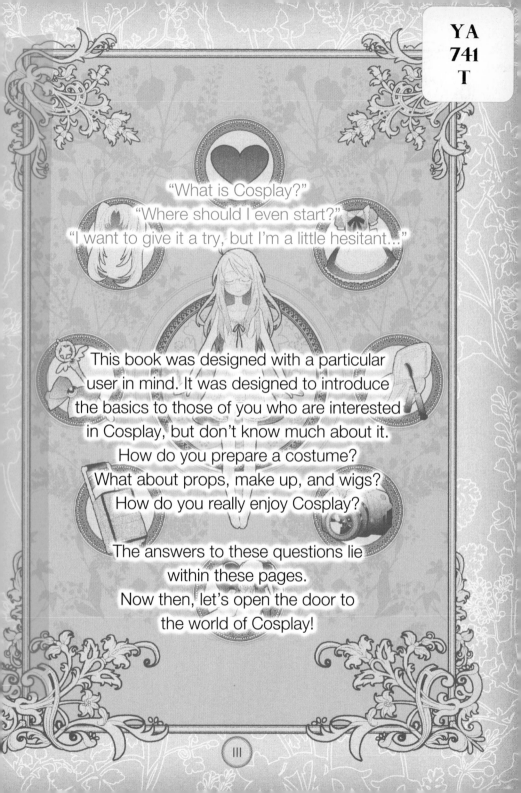

"What is Cosplay?"
"Where should I even start?"
"I want to give it a try, but I'm a little hesitant..."

This book was designed with a particular user in mind. It was designed to introduce the basics to those of you who are interested in Cosplay, but don't know much about it.
How do you prepare a costume?
What about props, make up, and wigs?
How do you really enjoy Cosplay?

The answers to these questions lie within these pages.
Now then, let's open the door to the world of Cosplay!

This book will teach you how to make the various parts of a costume. It will use the example of the imaginary character Magical Girl Luncasis's outfit. You could make a one piece dress like this out of different sorts of paper, but learning various methods for making the ribbons, corset, and boots will give you the skill-set you need to make whatever you want!

1. Sleeves

2. Hair Bows

3. Chest Bow

4. Large Bow for the Back

5. Corset

6. Wrist Decorations

7. One Piece Skirt

8. Decorated White Boots

1 Sleeves

A puffy sleeve tied with a red band. Finished with ruffles.

→ *Page 68*

2 Hair Bows

Easily clipped onto your styled hair. The bows for your wrists and shoes are made the same way.

→ *Page 77*

3 Chest Bow

The large jewel in the center can easily be separated from the bow it adorns. That way you can use it for other costumes as well!

→ *Page 73*

4 Large Bow for the Back

We used a deep pink satin for this, and it really makes for a gorgeous impression. The Chest bow is made in the same way.

→ *Page 76*

5 Corset

This is a three-colored corset with hooks and stiffeners added for stability. The shape will stay secure all day long.

→ *Page 70*

6 Wrist Decorations

This glossy chiffon material makes the wrist decorations really stand out.

→ *Page 80*

7 One Piece Skirt

Made from pink and light pink materials in two layers, the addition of lace really brings this puffy skirt to life.

→ *Page 65*

8 Decorated White Boots

We make these by making alterations to commercially available shoes. Choosing higher heels will help bring balance to the overall costume.

→ *Page 101*

Strike a Pose!

When deciding on your preferred pose for your character, it's useful to look through character materials and posters.

Also, consider the gender of the character you are playing. Male and female characters can give dramatically different impressions simply by changing the position of a fist or the way you plant your feet.

→ Page 178

——— Changing Eye Color ———

You can easily alter the color of your eyes with photo retouching software. It's a useful technique for those times when you can't put in contacts, or when you forget them.

→ *Page 185*

Step 1

Make a layer for your eye color, and zoom in on your eyes using the zoom tool. In the toolbox, select the "reverse background and foreground color" tool.

Step 2

When the color picker box opens, select the desired eye color and click okay. Use the brush tool to color your eyes.

Step 3

Change the layer mode from normal to screen.

Step 4

Your eyes are now colored!

Retouch Your Photos!

When you are ready to post your pictures online, or to make a business card, you can retouch your existing photos for even more impact. Adjusting brightness and contrast, as well as skin blemishes, marks, or wigs that aren't sitting right will help create exactly the mood you desire.

→ Page 183

Before

After

Model: Ayaka
Otsuka
Clothing Design: Rumine
Boot Production: Takasou
Wig Production: kic.
Photographer: Kazunori Igarashi
Photographic support: Mariko
Akiyama
Photography Studio:
Studio Rabbit Crown

CONTENTS

Prologue ·· 1

Chapter 1　How to Cosplay ··· 9

🌸　1-01　What is Cosplay? ··· 15

Who are Cosplayers? / Types of Cosplay / Different Cosplay Styles / What You Need to Cosplay

🌸　1-02　Having Fun Cosplaying! ································ 18

Enjoying Cosplay / Participating in Events / Spending Time with Your Friends / Communicating Online

🌸　Column　Frequently Asked Questions for Beginners ·········· 21

Chapter 2　How to Purchase and Arrange Your Costume　23

🌸　2-01　Buying a Costume ··· 33

Stores that Sell Cosplay Supplies / Buying Clothing Online / Using Online Auction Sites / Made to

Order Costumes / Price and Quality / What to Watch Out For

🌸　2-02　How to Rearrange Your Purchased Costume ·········· 36

About Alterations and Creations / Decide on the Alterations You Want to Make

🌸　2-03　Altering the Shapes and Sizes of Materials ·········· 37

Making borders with Bias Tape / Making Dart Adjustments / Adding or Altering Materials

🌸　2-04　Alerting Fabric ··· 40

Paints for the beginner / Spray Dyes / Using stencils to create patterns / Iron-on designs / Cutting

and Gluing Fabrics / The Best Fabrics for Pattern Making / The Best Gluing Procedures

🌸　Column　Links ··· 44

Chapter 3   Making a Costume Yourself 45

✿ 3-01   What You Need to Know 53

Decide on Your Concept / Basic Tools / Convenient Tools

✿ 3-02   Commonly Used Fabrics for Cosplaying 57

The Best Fabrics for Cosplaying / Fabrics Not Well-Suited for Cosplaying / About Adhesive Stiffeners

/ What to Watch for When Purchasing Fabric

✿ 3-03   How to Make Magic Girl Luncasis 62

Check over the Costume Design / Making the One Piece Dress / Making the Corset / Making the

Ribbon / Making Hair and Boot Decorations / Making the Wrist Decorations / Making the Choker

✿ 3-04   How to Take Care of Your Costume 84

How to Wash Your Costume / How to Store Your Costume

✿ Column   To Make or to Buy? 86

Chapter 4   Preparing Your Props 87

✿ 4-01   Using Pre-Existing Products 96

Buying Toys / Buying at a Specialty Store

✿ 4-02   Prop-Making and Common Materials 97

Foam Board / Styrofoam / Clay and Crystal Resin

✿ 4-03   How to Improve Shoes 100

Choosing the Shoes / Changing Shoe Color

✿ 4-04   Making Magic Girl Luncasis's Boots 101

Check the Design / Necessary Materials and Tools

✿ Column   Convenient Materials and Tools for Prop-Making 106

Chapter 5 Hair and Makeup 107

❀ 5 - 01 Makeup basics.. 115

Preparing for Makeup / Basic Makeup Process / Wigs and Makeup / Makeup Touch-Ups

❀ 5 - 02 Using Wigs 120

What is a Wig? / What to Watch Out for When Purchasing a Wig / How to Chose a Wig / How to Wear

a Wig / How to Style a Wig / How to Treat Your Wig / Items for Wigs

❀ 5 - 03 Color Contacts 131

How to Buy Color Contacts / How to Insert and Remove Color Contacts / During the Event /

Cleaning and Storing Your Contacts

❀ 5 - 04 Details 134

Makeup Other than Face Make up / Body Paint / Nails / Removing Unwanted Hair / Stockings /

Underwear / Exposure

❀ Column Hiding Your Breasts 138

Chapter 6 Participating in an Event 139

❀ 6 - 01 Deciding on an Event 149

Types of Events / What Makes an Event Easy to Participate In? / Things to Keep in Mind When

Deciding on an Event / Events Best Avoided by Beginners

❀ 6 - 02 What to Bring to the Event 153

What to Bring / How to Carry Your Costume / How to Carry Your Props / Business Cards

❀ 6 - 03 What Happens at the Event 157

How to Prepare for the Big Day / When You Arrive / Changing Into Your Costume / What to Watch Out

for in the Changing Room / Going to the Photography Area / What to Watch Out for When Taking

Pictures

❀ 6 - 04 What to Watch Out for at Events 162

Events Belong to Everyone / No Secret Pictures!

❀ Column Extra Advice 164

Chapter 7   Take Beautiful Pictures 165

❀ 7 - 01   How to Have Nice Pictures Taken 177
Good Places for Photography / About Lighting

❀ 7 - 02   The Basics of Cosplay Posing 178
Points to Remember / Think About How You Stand / Think About Your Hands / Use Your Costume /

Sitting Down Poses / Use Your Props / The Difference Between Girl and Boy Poses / Pair Poses

❀ 7 - 03   Retouching Photos 183
Retouching Basics / Adjusting the Brightness / Erasing Moles and Pimples / Skin Cleanup / Change

your Eye Color

❀ 7 - 04   Exhibiting Your Photos 187
Register with a Cosplay Community Site / Start a Blog or Website / What to Watch Out for on the

Internet

❀ Column   Facial Expressions 188

Epilogue 189

Afterword... 194

Prologue

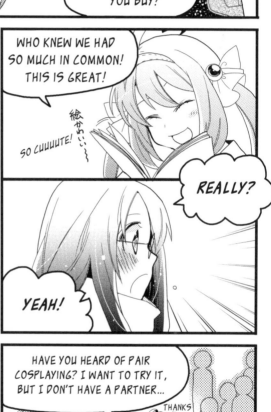

IT'S FUN TO DRESS UP AS YOUR FAVORITE CHARACTERS! YOU CAN GET OUT OF YOUR SHELL, AND MAKE FRIENDS WITH SIMILAR INTERESTS!

AND COSPLAYING IS SO DIFFERENT FROM NORMAL LIFE. YOU CAN HAVE ALL KINDS OF NEW EXPERIENCES AS YOUR CHARACTER!

WOW...

BUT I DON'T KNOW HOW TO START SOMETHING LIKE THAT...

THAT'S FINE!

7

8

How to Cosplay

❶ What is Cosplay?

❷ Having Fun Cosplaying!

COLUMN Frequently Asked Questions for Beginners

In this chapter, we will introduce you to the basics of Cosplaying. How many kinds of Cosplay are there? What do you need to do it? Where do people go when they want to Cosplay?

WELL, THERE ARE SPECIFIC COSPLAY EVENTS, WHICH ARE PROBABLY THE MAIN PLACES, BUT THERE ARE OFTEN COSPLAY AREAS AT COMIC EVENTS...

AND WHAT KIND OF EVENT ARE WE GOING TO PARTICIPATE IN?

AND THERE ARE COSPLAY DANCE PARTIES, AND COSPLAY PHOTOGRAPHY CLUBS.

WELL, WE WILL BE PAIR COSPLAYING AT...

CHIKA-COURSE THIS SUMMER!

CHIKA-COURSE?

1-01 | What is Cosplay?

In this chapter, we will introduce you to the basics of Cosplaying. How many types of Cosplay are there? What do you need to do it? Where do people go when they want to Cosplay?

Who are Cosplayers?

Cosplay is short for "costume play." This generally refers to people who normally dress up as characters from anime, manga, or video games. People who do Cosplay at various events are called "Cosplayers" by others, but they often refer to themselves as "players."

Types of Cosplay

The following are the main types of Cosplay:

◆ Imaginary Characters

Here the Cosplayer aims to recreate the clothes, hair, and items carried by anime, manga, and video game characters. This book's major focus is on this type of Cosplaying.

◆ Clothes that Exist in Reality

This is what we call it when you wear uniforms of certain professionals, like the military, the costumes of famous pop stars, or other clothing that you wouldn't typically wear.

◆ Original Costumes

This is what we call it when you create your own original costume designs. Often this takes the form of Lolita costume play, or Gothic dresses. There are people that wear these cloths outside of events, just when walking around town, as a form of entertainment.

Different Cosplay Styles

This book mainly focuses on Cosplaying imaginary characters. But within that there are still other styles to examine.

◆ Imaginary Cosplay

This type of Cosplay aims to recreate an imaginary character through makeup and costumes.

◆ Joke Cosplay

This Cosplay aims to make others laugh through intentional jokes or by the character chosen.

◆ Hero Cosplay

This includes rangers and other heros that often have their faces hidden with masks.

◆ Robot Cosplay

Here the Cosplayer covers their entire body with robotic like parts. In Japanese they are also known as *Kigurumi*.

◆ CHAKUGURUMI Cosplay

This style covers the Cosplayer's whole body in costume. Often Cosplayers wear an anime face mask, too. They often appear at character shows. In Japan they are also known as "Dora."

❊ What You Need to Cosplay

The following items are usually used in Cosplaying:

◆ Clothing

◆ Props

◆ Makeup

◆ Wigs

◆ Suitcase (To Carry Your Costume)

◆ Digital Camera

1−02 | Having Fun Cosplaying!

Cosplaying is more than just wearing a costume, it's also participating in events. Both the participation and the preparations are fun. Let's take a look at the sort of events that people participate in when they are Cosplaying.

✿ Enjoying Cosplay

Cosplay is fun in a lot of ways besides just dressing up. Let's look at what is involved in the whole process, from preparations to participation.

1. Research	It's fun to think about what kind of character you want to become. It's fun to imagine the concrete ways you will try to recreate that character. The more you think about the specifics the more fun you have.
2. Preparing Your Costume	It's fun to imagine the way you will make your costume. It may cost money and it may be difficult at times, but the more you put into it the more you will get out of it. Furthermore, if you decide to make the costume yourself, you'll get to savor the process of its construction.
3. Communication	By participating in Cosplay events, you'll be able to meet many people who share the same hobbies as yourself. There are Cosplay communities online as well.
4. Taking Pictures	If you take pictures of yourself and others when you are Cosplaying, not only will it give you something to remember the experience, but you'll naturally want to take better pictures in the future. Cosplay doesn't have to end when the event ends. By looking through pictures afterward, you make sure that your costume and character are balanced. You can come up with ideas for better poses. Pictures will help you to improve your Cosplay technique.

Participating in Events

Participating in events is one of the main goals of Cosplay. Here we introduce the main types of events.

Cosplay Events	These are events that are held specifically for Cosplaying. Not only do Cosplayers go, but photographers are also often found here.
Comic Con Events	The big Comic Con events attract a lot of Cosplayers. There are events that are genre-specific, and those that are free for original Cosplaying. There are often spaces reserved at Comic Con events specifically for Cosplaying.
Cosplay Dance Parties	These are events to Cosplay and dance at the same time. There is normally a DJ and a stage. They do not only play music from anime and video games, but also Eurobeat and Techno.
Cosplay Photography Events	These are events for Cosplayers and photographers to meet and take pictures. They are often held in rented out photography studios. Participation is normally limited to small groups, and the skill level tends to be quite high.

The following sites are great for looking up Cosplay events:

◆ **animecons.com**

◆ **cosplay.com**

◆ **cosplayhouse.com**

In addition to the sites mentioned above, there are also many other Cosplay community sites out there that you are sure to find useful.

Spending Time With Your Friends

By participating in Cosplay events, you can meet many people who share similar hobbies with you. When doing so, try to keep the following in mind:

- Greet people.

- Even if you get involved in a great conversation, it's best to keep it to a few minutes.

- Exchange business cards with others.

Greeting people is just what it sounds like. You say hello or good morning to others. When parting ways, you should congratulate others on a job well done.

It is best to avoid long conversations because Cosplayers often participate in large groups. By starting a long conversation, you don't want to annoy others in that person's group, or keep a photographer waiting. It's fine to introduce yourself simply at the event, and send them a text or email later on. This is also why business cards come in handy.

Communicating Online

By participating in online communities, you will be able to enjoy Cosplay outside of actual events.

◆ cosplay.com

◆ gaiaonline.com

These sites give you access to not only a community, but also information on events and shopping and supplies. A quick internet search will produce multiple websites that have online Cosplay communities.

Frequently Asked Questions for Beginners

When you are first starting out, you might be confused or nervous. You don't have to do all of it at once. Take it slow and ease yourself into the wide world of Cosplay one step at a time. Here we aim to answer some questions that beginners often have.

Q: I am interested in Cosplaying a minor character. Is that all right?

A: If you are really interested in a certain character, it doesn't matter how famous they are. You may feel down when others don't recognize the character, but when you meet someone who does, the joy you feel will make up for it.

Q: I'm short. Should I not dress up as masculine characters?

A: Don't worry. Dress up as the character you like. Depending on the costume, you may be able to make up for it with your shoes.

Q: I'm tall, but I want to dress up as a small character.

A: This is hard to make up for with a costume, but when you take pictures you can sit or kneel to make yourself look smaller than you actually are.

Q: I don't know how to make costumes. Is it all right to use one that is commercially available?

A: Yes. And just because a costume is cheap doesn't mean it will be of poor quality. What is important is your desire to participate. Even still, if something seems too cheap to be true, it probably is. If all you worry about is the price, in the end Cosplay will just be wearing the clothes of a character. What you want to think of is how you should go about becoming that character. Make sure that your costume and props are good enough to make you feel that you have become the person you want to be. Chapters 2 and 3 further discuss clothing and props.

Q: I'd like to keep my costume secret from my family…

A: When purchasing a costume over the phone or internet, you can have it sent to your place of employment, or tell them that you will pick it up at the post office. You may also request that the package be labeled "Accessories" or "Clothing," so that it will not be apparent that you are purchasing the goods for Cosplaying.

Q: Is Cosplaying only for anime and video game characters?

A: Of course not. People also dress up as characters from movies, TV, novels, bands, as pop stars, comedians, commercial characters, military personnel , politicians, famous people, historical figures, religious figures, and other things. However, there are events that prohibit costumes of public services (police, firefighters, military, etc.). Also some Gothic, Lolita, and visual-kei groups have their own rules.

Q: How should I protect my clothes, weapons, and armor?

A: If you have articles that cannot be washed, at least disinfect the fabric parts. Armor and weapons and things that are easy to break should be stored in cardboard boxes along with packing peanuts or bubble wrap.

Q: What is Awase Cosplay?

A: It's when a group decides on a theme and everyone dresses in accordance with it. Usually it is done among friends, but you may see groups on the internet recruiting members.

You may be nervous at first, but the most important thing is to love your character and to really want to recreate them! It's okay to take it one-step at a time. Have fun!

Chapter 2

How to Purchase and Arrange Your Costume

❶ Buying a Costume

❷ How to Rearrange Your Purchased Costume

❸ Altering the Shapes and Sizes of Materials

❹ Altering Fabric

COLUMN Links

You need a costume if you want to Cosplay. Here we detail what to keep in mind when purchasing one, how to rearrange it, and introduce good stores for Cosplay shopping.

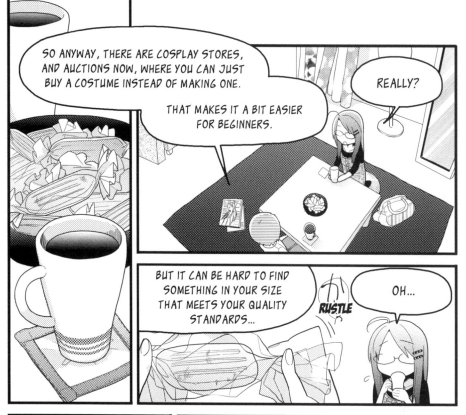

SO ANYWAY, THERE ARE COSPLAY STORES, AND AUCTIONS NOW, WHERE YOU CAN JUST BUY A COSTUME INSTEAD OF MAKING ONE.

THAT MAKES IT A BIT EASIER FOR BEGINNERS.

REALLY?

BUT IT CAN BE HARD TO FIND SOMETHING IN YOUR SIZE THAT MEETS YOUR QUALITY STANDARDS...

RUSTLE

OH...

AREN'T THERE PLACES THAT WILL MAKE A COSTUME FOR YOU?

AHHH

AN ORDER-MADE ONE? SURE...

WELL IF YOU ORDER ONE, IT WILL CERTAINLY FIT WELL, AND BE HIGH QUALITY...

BUT THERE IS NO GUARANTEE THAT THE MAKER WILL BE FAMILIAR WITH THE DESIGN YOU WANT!

CRUNCH

CRUNCH

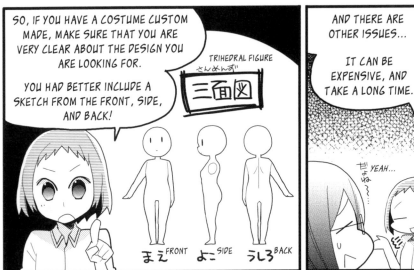

SO, IF YOU HAVE A COSTUME CUSTOM MADE, MAKE SURE THAT YOU ARE VERY CLEAR ABOUT THE DESIGN YOU ARE LOOKING FOR.

YOU HAD BETTER INCLUDE A SKETCH FROM THE FRONT, SIDE, AND BACK!

TRIHEDRAL FIGURE
さんめんず
三面図

まえ FRONT　よこ SIDE　うしろ BACK

AND THERE ARE OTHER ISSUES...

IT CAN BE EXPENSIVE, AND TAKE A LONG TIME.

甘いよね…… YEAH...

I GUESS I REALLY WOULD RATHER LEARN TO MAKE A COSTUME ON MY OWN...

LOOK, YOU CAN JUST ALTER A PREEXISTING MAID COSTUME TO APPROXIMATE LUNCASIS!

I'LL HELP YOU OUT! IT'LL BE EASY!

UH... OKAY!

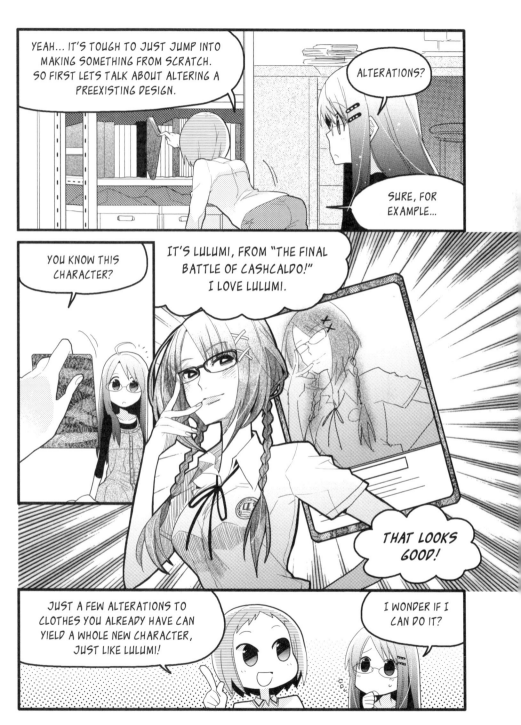

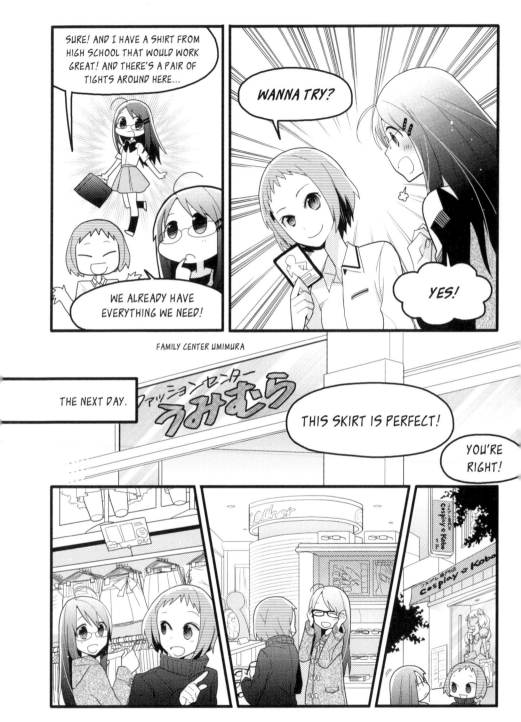

FAMILY CENTER UMIMURA

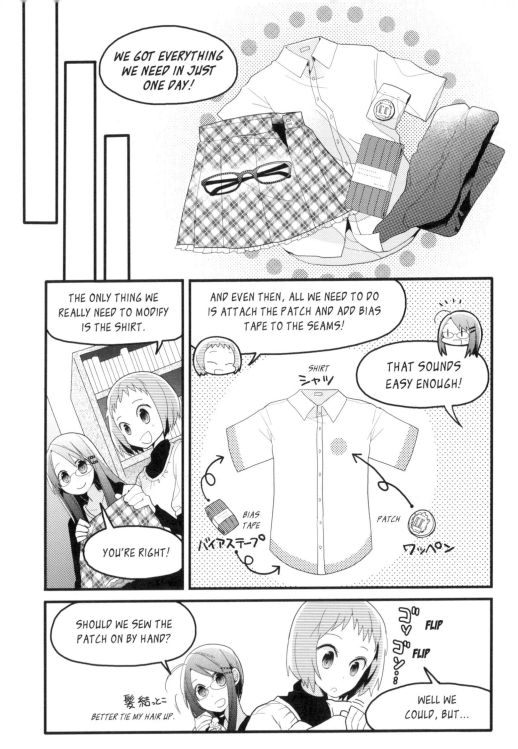

WE GOT EVERYTHING WE NEED IN JUST ONE DAY!

THE ONLY THING WE REALLY NEED TO MODIFY IS THE SHIRT.

YOU'RE RIGHT!

AND EVEN THEN, ALL WE NEED TO DO IS ATTACH THE PATCH AND ADD BIAS TAPE TO THE SEAMS!

THAT SOUNDS EASY ENOUGH!

SHIRT
シャツ

BIAS TAPE
バイアステープ

PATCH
ワッペン

SHOULD WE SEW THE PATCH ON BY HAND?

髪結っとこ
BETTER TIE MY HAIR UP.

FLIP
FLIP

WELL WE COULD, BUT...

IT'S EASIER TO JUST USE A FABRIC GLUE TO STICK IT ON!

FABRIC GLUE

手芸ボンド
布用

YOU CAN USE GLUE?!

うんっ
YUP, YOU JUST NEED TO MAKE SURE YOU KNOW WHERE YOU WANT IT TO GO.

できた!
I DID IT!

HOW ABOUT THE BIAS TAPE? CAN WE GLUE THAT ON TOO?

BIAS TAPE
ふちどりさん

THERE ARE TYPES MADE FOR USE WITH GLUES OR SELF-ADHESIVES, BUT SEWING IT ON ALWAYS WORKS BETTER.

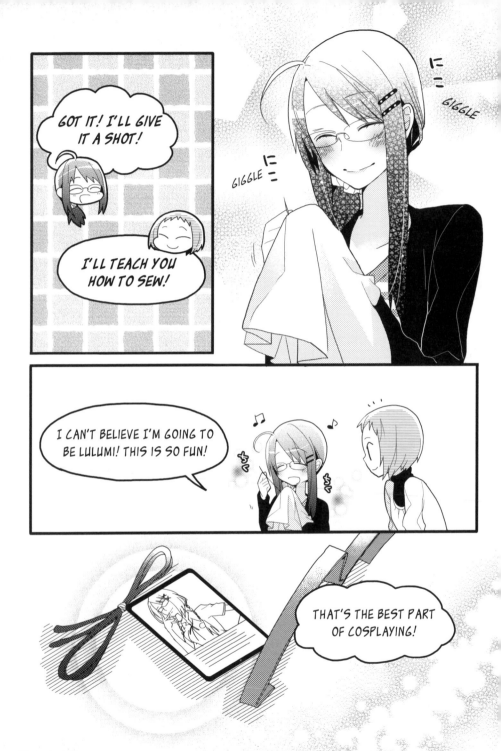

GIGGLE

GIGGLE

GOT IT! I'LL GIVE IT A SHOT!

I'LL TEACH YOU HOW TO SEW!

I CAN'T BELIEVE I'M GOING TO BE LULUMI! THIS IS SO FUN!

THAT'S THE BEST PART OF COSPLAYING!

Chapter

2-01 | Buying a Costume

You need a costume if you want to Cosplay. If it is possible to purchase a costume for the character you want to be, it's much easier to jump into the world of Cosplay.

Stores That Sell Cosplay Supplies

The following stores sell Cosplay products:

◆ cosplayhouse.com

◆ cosplayfu.com

◆ cosplaymagic.com

Keep in mind that most Cosplay shops won't let you try on the costume before you purchase it. If you want more information about the materials or design, you will need to ask the seller directly.

Buying Clothing Online

There are many online retailers selling costumes. While it's true that you cannot see the actual product when you are shopping online, these shops often have a wonderful selection of characters:

◆ cosplayfu.com

◆ cosplaymagic.com

◆ cosplayhouse.com

◆ cosplayshopper.com

◆ hellocosplay.com

Using Online Auction Sites

You can find many custom-made costumes on online auction sites. There are many costumes available, but it can be difficult to discern the quality, and it can be difficult to know if the costume is going to fit. Try to read the descriptions, do not buy based solely on the picture. Whether purchasing from a domestic or foreign seller, there is a chance the product may be of questionable quality. Make sure to check the seller's rating, and give the purchase a lot of thought before you bid.

Made to Order Costumes

Even if the costume you want is not being sold commercially, you may be able to have it custom-made. This is normally done by an experienced group of Cosplayers or by fashion specialists. To get started, you'll first need a diagram of the design you want. It's best to have as much information as possible to give to the maker. Give them this information when you ask for an estimate and be sure to tell them what materials and shapes you are looking for. Be specific!

Make sure that you get your measurements first. It's ideal if the person doing the measurements will also be making the costume. The more you compile the design, the more measurements will be necessary.

Keep in mind that having costumes made to order costs time and money. It is also not uncommon for it to take a few months for the process, so make sure that you begin ordering well before you need the costume.

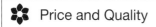

Price and Quality

Even when separate costumes are for the same character, the difference in price can be surprising. The most typical reason for this is the quality of material and the care put into the construction.

The following table should give you a good idea of what to expect from each price point:

Price	Quality and Features
$50 and under	This price point usually includes foreign-made items for popular characters. At this price point poorly made items are not uncommon.
$50-$300	Most costumes fall into this category. For items under 300 dollars, the sellers generally set their own prices; therefore, it is best to carefully inspect the product when purchasing.
$300 and up	In this category, specialist-made and costumes made by groups tend to cost in excess of $300. They are typically very high quality and they recreate the character design well. You can be relatively assured of the quality, but keep in mind that expensive does not necessarily guarantee quality.

What to Watch Out For

As we have said before, most shops will not let you try on the costumes before purchasing them. When you are shopping online you only have the photographs and written information to go by. Whether you buy in person or online, you will have to make a decision based on appearances. Here's what to watch out for when doing so:

◆ **Details of the costume are correct.**

◆ **Fabrics suit the character.**

◆ **Quality of the materials (cotton, polyester).**

◆ **How the shop is regarded and reviewed.**

Aside from the above points, you will want to check the stitching to ensure it is of high quality. If you are inexperienced in purchasing costumes, bring along someone to give you advice. It will make the whole process simpler.

Check the design.

Check the quality and the colors.

Check the materials.

Read the shop's reviews.

2-02 | How to Rearrange Your Purchased Costume

Before you try to make a costume from scratch, why not start off with making alterations to pre-existing costumes? It is a much simpler way to get started Cosplaying.

About Alterations and Creations

Cosplaying involves many different designs and stitches that you don't encounter when making more traditional clothing. Of course, it is better if you are an experienced tailor, but many Cosplayers simply find their own way of doing things.

Why not start with a costume that you can purchase for around $100, and slowly, over time, make improvements to it? You may even be able to start with your normal clothing.

Simple alterations do not require the use of any special tools.

School uniforms can become a character's costume with a few easy modifications.

Decide on the Alterations You Want to Make

By making alterations to little parts of the costume, you can change the overall impression quite simply. The main alterations are as follows:

◆ Shape (design, silhouette)

◆ Size (alterations for a perfect fit)

◆ Materials (additions, alterations)

◆ Color

Take a moment to consider how to best utilize pre-existing designs and costumes. Take a note of the areas to be altered, or consider drawing an illustration to get your ideas organized. We will go over the most common alterations in the next chapter.

2−03 | Altering the Shapes and Sizes of Materials

When the details of a design seem a bit off, simple alterations can fix them. When the size in certain areas needs adjusting, pleats can fix most problems.

 ## Making Borders with Bias Tape

◆ What is Bias tape?

Bias tape is sold at most fabric and sewing shops. It is often used for hemming and making borders by Cosplayers. There are different shapes and sizes, and all can be used to alter the impression of your costume. Bias tape is sold in both single-fold and double-fold styles.

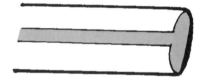

Single-Fold Tape

Double-Fold Tape

The double-fold style is more common, but the single-fold style is more appropriate for Cosplaying.

◆ How To Use Bias Tape:

Bias tape can be either self-adhesive or iron on. Tape without adhesive must either be glued or sewn onto the clothing. So then, how do you use double-fold style bias tape with glue? The next page contains detailed instructions.

① Sandwich the end of the cloth in bias tape to determine the best position.

② Apply glue to one side of the tape, press to the cloth, and allow it to dry.

③ Apply glue to the remaining side of the tape, press to the cloth.

It is important not to stretch the tape tightly when you are gluing it down. Bias tape can be quite elastic, so if you pull it tight before gluing it will result in wrinkles in the final costume.

A sewing machine can also be used to produce even better results. Sewing may also be done by hand.

Making Dart Adjustments

Often, purchased costumes don't fit exactly the way you would like them to. By adding darts (or adjusting pre-existing ones) sizes can be altered to a certain extent.

Darts are three-dimensional pleats added to the fabric where you would like it to hug your body closer. Depending on the type of clothing, often many darts are added.

If the clothing is too tight, the darts can be removed. If the clothing is loose, the darts can be refolded and sewn again. By tightening or loosening up to 4 cm, the silhouette of the costume can be altered.

Here we see an area that contains darts.

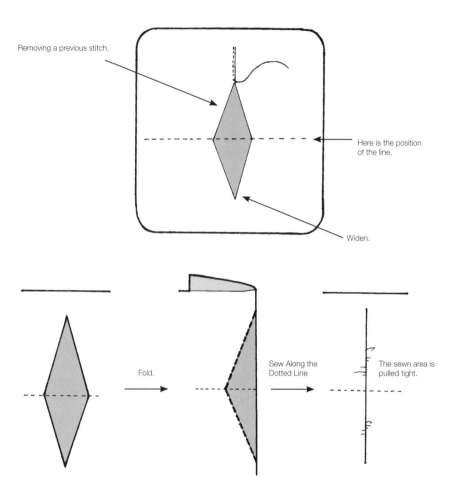

Removing a previous stitch.

Here is the position of the line.

Widen.

Fold.

Sew Along the Dotted Line

The sewn area is pulled tight.

🌸 Adding or Altering Materials

By adding props or accessories to pre-existing costumes, the overall impression of a costume can be altered dramatically.

By adding patches, buttons, or pockets, a whole new costume can emerge.

These little details can bring a mediocre costume to life. Belts, jewelry, scarves, lace, etc... By introducing new materials to the design, the quality of the whole costume improves.

2-04 | Altering Fabric

Adding patterns to a pre-existing costume is a simple alteration that makes a big impact. Let's take a look at how this is best accomplished.

Paints for the Beginner

If you are going to dye the fabrics, you must keep the materials and original color in mind. Polyester costumes require a special dye made for polyester. Furthermore, if the original color is dark, the dye might not be able to fully cover it. It is much easier to start with a white, or lightly colored costume. There are many different types of paintable dyes, but here is a list of the simplest to use for beginners.

When using dyes make sure to work in a well-ventilated space.

◆ Dye for Vinyl

This dye is used for drawing on tents and other vinyl surfaces. Because of its versatility, it is also great for drawing on other objects, like boots.

◆ Paintable Dye

This dye is very easy to use, much like you would use simple paints. The colors can even be blended and used. Once the dye has dried, you simply iron over it to adhere it to the fabric. When ironing, you should sandwich a spare piece of cloth between the iron and the pattern you've drawn.

✿ Spray Dyes

Spray dye doesn't ooze or drip, making it useful for dying specific areas. It can be difficult to dye a darkly colored fabric with sprays, however.

✿ Using Stencils to Create Patterns

When using spray dyes, stencils can help create a perfect pattern. Use paper or masking tape to cover the areas you don't want to dye. Stencils are indispensable for creating your final design.

1. Draw the design you want to dye on paper.

You can also use a computer to print out the design.

2. Cover the back of the design with double-sided tape.

Make sure the tape extends past the borders of the design.

3. Cut out the design.

Cut as carefully as you can. The cut area becomes the design.

4. Tape the stencil down to the desired part of the fabric.

If the stencil floats, the design will be blurry. Make sure it is flat on the fabric.

5. Cover the rest of the fabric with newspaper.

Protect the rest of the costume from the spray dye.

6. Spray over the stencil.

Hold the spray about a meter over the stencil and apply the spray evenly. Don't put it on too thick. You can always add another layer.

❀ Iron On Designs

Many paper companies sell iron on
printing papers designed to be used
with an inkjet printer.

Make a design on your computer,
print it onto the special paper, and the
design can be attached to fabric with
an iron.

You can add design elements that are difficult to achieve with paints, like gradients.

However, compared to paints, the resulting colors are light, and the papers don't work well with

polyester.

❀ Cutting and Gluing Fabrics

You can also make patterns without paints, by simply
attaching other fabrics to the costume. Because the
design can be cut and checked before it has to be
attached, this method often produces better results
than dyes.

Furthermore, by using different materials, it is easy to
quickly and dramatically alter the overall impression of
a costume. Silver and gold artificial leathers can add a
metallic flair to a design quite simply.

Make sure to glue in a well-ventilated place.

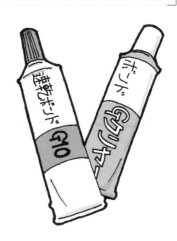

The Best Fabrics for Pattern Making

◆ Velour

Velour is a great velvet-like fabric. It is often used to line jewelry
boxes. It is easy to cut and use, and it quickly and simply
adds an air of refinement to a costume. Great for neckties and
ribbons, those single accessories that really set off a design.
When used for adding patterns to costumes it adds a rich, royal
impression.

◆ Artificial Leathers and Enamels

Both leatherettes and enamels are artificial fabrics. Matte
finished fabrics are leatherette and glossy fabrics are enamel.

Simple applications to boots and belts can make a dramatic contribution to the feeling of a
costume.

Velour, leatherette, and enamel are all best applied with adhesive. When sewing velour, spraying
the thread with silicone spray, or running paper through the sewing machine along with the fabric
will make the process much simpler.

All of them are great fabrics, but they are all very difficult to smooth out once they wrinkle. Also,
they cannot be washed in a washing machine.

 # The Best Gluing Procedures

Badges and accessories for Cosplay can also be attached with
adhesives and glues.

When attaching them, first temporarily secure them with tape, then
take a step back to double check the positioning. If you take the
time to check the balance of the positioning, you will end up with a
better final design.

Links

There are a lot of online stores that sell a variety of costumes and props. We've listed a few below. We do not hold any associations or connections to the shops below. This list is meant simply as a sampling of different sellers available. Use caution and prudent judgment when shopping.

◆ mooncostumes.com

◆ cosplayfu.com

◆ cosplaymagic.com

◆ cosplayhouse.com

◆ cosplayshopper.com

◆ hellocosplay.com

◆ cosplay.com

◆ cosplaysushi.com

◆ xcoser.com

It's easy to call something a "cosplay store," but in reality there are many different kinds of stores! All of them have their own unique qualities and specialties, so when you decide to buy a costume, it might be a good idea to ask to see samples of their previous designs.
It's lots of fun just to browse these stores online.

Chapter 3 Making a Costume Yourself

- ❶ What You Need to Know
- ❷ Commonly Used Fabrics for Cosplaying
- ❸ How to Make Magic Girl Luncasis
- ❹ How to Take Care of Your Costume
- COLUMN To Make or to Buy?

While it is more difficult to make your own costume, it is also more fun and more pleasing to have a costume that you made yourself. Make sure you have the knowledge, preparation, and tools that you need, and try to make your own costume! This chapter also includes information on how to take care of your completed costume.

I HAVE A BUNCH OF BOOKS ON LUNE LOVELY!

I EVEN HAVE A CHARACTER REFERENCE BOOK!

THUD!

WOW, IT'S GREAT THAT YOU ARE SO DEDICATED!

YOU KNOW THAT CHARACTER DESIGNS CAN CHANGE A BIT DEPENDING ON WHERE YOU ARE PULLING THEM FROM.

LIKE WHETHER IT'S FROM THE ANIME SERIES OR THE ORIGINAL MANGA. YOU'RE GOING TO NEED TO DECIDE WHERE YOU WANT TO TAKE THE CHARACTER FROM.

I GUESS SO.

THE LUNE LOVELY DESIGNS CHANGED A BIT BETWEEN THE MANGA AND ANIME VERSIONS. THE PARTS ARE IN DIFFERENT PLACES, AND THE COLORS ARE A BIT DIFFERENT TOO.

I THINK THE DESIGNS ARE A BIT MORE COMPLICATED IN THE MANGA VERSION THOUGH...

ANIMATED VERSION

MANGA VERSION

SO LET'S TRY OUR HAND AT THE ANIME CHARACTER DESIGNS!

THEY SHOULD BE A LITTLE EASIER.

MATERIALS...

HEY RIKO, YOU'VE MADE A BUNCH OF COSTUMES BEFORE, RIGHT?

部屋にも沢山あたし'''
I SAW A BUNCH IN YOUR ROOM SO...

HOW DO YOU KEEP COSTUMES NICE AFTER THEY ARE MADE?

TADA!

キ チ!

WELL JUST LIKE WITH NORMAL CLOTHES, YOU BASICALLY WANT TO FOLD THEM NICELY AND PUT THEM AWAY.

BUT SOME MATERIALS WILL BE RUINED IF THEY GET WRINKLED, SO FOR THOSE COSTUMES, I KEEP A PLACE IN MY CLOSET TO HANG THEM UP.

ハイミロンとか
合皮とか
LIKE HYMILON OR LEATHERETTE

WHAT ABOUT GETTING THEM TO AND FROM AN EVENT?

LOT'S OF PEOPLE USE A SUITCASE, LIKE THEY WERE GOING ON VACATION!

THAT WAY YOU CAN KEEP YOUR PROPS AND MATERIALS ALL TOGETHER!

BE CAREFUL WHEN YOU ARE CARRYING THEM!

持ち運びには注意してねっ

* SEE CHAPTER 6 FOR TIPS ON CARRYING A SUITCASE DURING RUSH HOUR.

CAN YOU JUST WASH A COSTUME LIKE NORMAL CLOTHES?

NORMALLY WE TRY TO WASH THEM BY HAND, BUT IF YOU CAN'T DO THAT RIGHT AWAY,

JUST HANG THEM UP NEAR A WINDOW, OR IN A ROOM WITH GOOD VENTILATION.

I GUESS HANDMADE COSTUMES SHOULD BE WASHED BY HAND THEN, HUH?

AND DEPENDING ON THE MATERIAL OR THE QUALITY, YOU MIGHT NOT BE ABLE TO WASH A COSTUME AT ALL!

WHATEVER YOU DO, DON'T LET A COSTUME SIT AROUND WHEN IT IS WET, YOU HAVE TO HANG IT UP!

DON'T LEAVE IT OUT WET!
放置せず

HANG IT UP!
すぐ干す!!

WHAT DO YOU DO WITH A COSTUME THAT YOU CAN'T WASH?

IF YOU CAN'T WASH IT, THEN DISINFECT AND DEODORIZE IT BEFORE HANGING IT UP IN YOUR ROOM TO AIR OUT.

OKAY...

NOW THEN, READY TO MAKE A COSTUME?!

THERE'S SO MUCH TO LEARN!

YOU'LL FIGURE IT ALL OUT SOON ENOUGH!

お、

Y...YES PLEASE!

52

Chapter 3-01 | What You Need to Know

When it comes time to make your own costume from scratch, you are going to need a lot of tools. But there is no need to get them all right from the get go! Just buy what is needed when the need arises.

Decide on Your Concept

◆ Is it an Original Creation or an Anime Character?

Before you get down to making your costume, make sure you know exactly what it is you want to make. Anime, manga, television, and video game characters may show up all over the place, but they differ in their details. Decide what your standards and priorities are before you start making the costume. You can always start with an easy design, just to get going.

When Cosplaying anime and manga characters, there are often official guides to the character and what they carry that will come in handy. These guides are useful even if you are just making alterations to a pre-existing costume.

◆ Figurines

If the character has an official figurine available, it would be wise to purchase it. The figurines are useful because they are three-dimensional. You may not be used to seeing the character from behind, or in profile. The figurines give you a good idea of the whole character and make the costume design process much simpler.

Basic Tools

The following basic tools will be necessary.

Name	Price
Measuring Tape (made of something flexible)	$ 3.00
Needles (various sizes, at least three)	$ 2.00
Chalk Pencil (vanishes with time, 2 or 3 colors)	$ 2.00
Thread (white, black, and red are basic. For hand and machine sewing)	$ 2.00

Ruler (One meter ruler and one 30 cm ruler)	$ 10.00
Scissors (thread cutters and fabric splitters)	$ 15.00
Iron (a steam iron is best)	$ 45.00
Sewing Machine (home use)	$ 200.00

It is much more convenient to use a sewing machine, but costumes can also be made by hand. There are many experienced Cosplayers who make their costumes by hand. If you are going to buy a machine, a simple home model is sufficient. There is no need to buy an expensive computerized one. If you feel like getting a better machine buy a professional or Serger machine, you should prepare three needles for thin, normal, and thick cloths.

Chalk pencils will vanish with time, leaving the cloth clean and the costume looking good. Thread can be bought cheaply, but cheap thread breaks quickly and leads to problems in the long run. We recommend buying your thread at a sewing shop, and getting a reasonably strong one to work with. You will also want to have some fabric glues at hand.

Convenient Tools

There are other tools that are not necessary, but convenient to have available. There is no need to get them immediately, but you might consider purchasing them with time.

◆ Professional Sewing and Lock Sewing Machines

With a professional or lock machine, leatherette and other difficult to work with materials can be sewn easily.

Professional Sewing machine

This is for sewing straight lines. It's good at sewing leatherette or other thick materials. It can also sew fasteners onto boots.

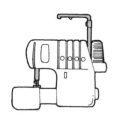

Serger Machine

Prevents frayed edges by creating end stitches. Can easily add frills to dresses.

◆ Silk Pin

This is a very thin pin so that the cloth is not damaged. It can even be run through a sewing machine, as the silk pin will break if hit by the needle, instead of the sewing machine. It's usually sold as 100 packs for around three dollars. They cannot really be used with thick fabrics, but works great with velour, leather, and polyester.

◆ Full-Length Mirror

With one of these, you can see your whole costume and check it's fit at one time. It's not rare to have a costume where all the parts are great, but the overall balance is off. For example, a costume's waist could sit and inch or two above your own.

◆ Tailor's Torso

This is very convenient for getting an objective idea of your overall design. There are also special Tailor Torsos designed just for displaying your design, but these are often short, and unable to be stuck with pins, so it's better to get a standard Torso.

◆ Computer and Printer

There are internet sites that feature downloadable designs for use in Cosplay. They can be printed out and applied to costumes. When applying designs to costumes, avoid using scotch tape, as it can stick to the fabric and ruin it. We recommend masking tape.

◆ Tracing Paper and Craft paper

This thin, see-through paper is great for copying designs you find in magazines or in photographs.

◆ Needle Disposal

Cutters and needles often break for safety, but leaving them sitting around is dangerous. There are disposal boxes made specifically for storing these dangerous items, and they are readily available.

◆ Adhesives

Aside from superglue, there are other adhesives that are commonly used in the Cosplaying community, like instant adhesives and hot glue (glue gun).

Instant adhesives can be used on most materials, but the trick is to use a very small amount. If the adhesive does not harden fast enough, you can accelerate the process using an instant adhesive hardening accelerator (spray). This will normally set the adhesive within a number of seconds.

Hot glue is a hard type of adhesive that is melted with heat using a glue gun. The materials can easily be found at a big box store. When using a glue gun, be very careful not to burn yourself. Also keep in mind that the adhesive may melt again if exposed to high temperatures.

Craft and fabric stores carry a wide range of different textiles, though not all of them will be useful for Cosplaying. This section will take a closer look at the most useful textiles for Cosplaying.

 ## The Best Fabrics for Cosplaying

Sometimes costumes are brought to events folded and stored in bags. Because of this, the best fabrics are those that do not wrinkle easily. You also must learn to think of fabrics for more than just their appearance, as some are easier to use than others. Here we introduce the fabrics most applicable for Cosplaying.

◆ Polyester Twill

This is thick and difficult to wrinkle. It is often used for uniforms and military themes.

◆ Urban Twill

This is very similar in appearance and use to polyester, though slightly thicker. It is often available in a wider variety of colors than polyester.

◆ Poly/Cotton Broadcloth Blend

This is often used to make uniform blouses. It is very thin, and great for making frills.

◆ Amunzen

This is a light polyester, excellent for dresses. It doesn't wrinkle easily, and forms good drapes. It is less glossy than satin, and is easy to dye bright colors.

◆ Velour

This is a fuzzy fabric that gives a rich impression. It is used for accessories like boots and jewelry and ribbons just as often as it is used for clothing.

◆ Velveteen

Fuzzy, like Velour, and appears very similar to it.

◆ Leatherette

An artificial fabric designed to look like leather. There are many different kinds available. When choosing leatherette, look at its thickness and color, and choose it much like you would fresh fruit at a supermarket. The backside of leatherette does not slide through sewing machines very well, so spraying your thread with silicone, or using a Teflon foot will help.

◆ Tulle Netting

Used to add volume to skirts or to make Paniers. There are soft tulles and hard tulles, their thickness designated by a number. #50 and above will keep shape well. There are many varieties and thicknesses. It is excellent for producing western-themed clothing.

◆ Lion Board

Not really a fabric, but the thinnest ones can be sewn with a sewing machine, and it is excellent for producing collars or hats. For when adhesive stiffeners will not work properly to hold the desired shape, thin Styrofoam boards will do the trick.

Fabrics Not Well Suited for Cosplay

There are many common, popular fabrics that are not too easy to work with when Cosplaying. We recommend using the fabrics we have already listed, but as a reference, we include the following list of fabrics that you should try to avoid.

◆ 100% Cotton Sheeting

Almost always available at craft shops, but because it is designed for crafts, it is thin and very easy to wrinkle. It is not well suited for clothing.

◆ 100% Cotton Satin

There're many types of satin, but 100% cotton satin ends up looking tacky and cheap. It is best avoided.

◆ 100% Cotton Velvet

Similar to velour or velveteen, but shows dirt and wrinkles immediately, and is more difficult to work with. Best avoided unless you are very experienced.

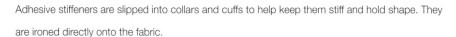

About Adhesive Stiffeners

Adhesive stiffeners are slipped into collars and cuffs to help keep them stiff and hold shape. They are ironed directly onto the fabric.
Thin stiffeners are available for thin fabrics and thicker stiffeners are best used with thicker fabrics.

Your iron should be set to a medium temperature setting. If you rub the iron over the stiffener when applying it, it will stretch and end up producing wrinkles. They are best applied by allowing the iron to sit still on one spot at a time. If you move from the center toward the edges of the stiffener, you can avoid troubling bubbles getting under the surface.

What to Watch for When Purchasing Fabric

You can purchase your fabrics online, or in person at a store. Regardless, you will have the shop cut the fabric to the size and amount you require. Before you go shopping, make sure you know how much fabric you will need. If you purchase more than you need, you won't have to go shopping again in the event of an accident or mistake.

When purchasing fabrics, make sure you take the width measurement into account as well as the length. Typical widths are 90, 110, and 140 cm. For the same length of fabric, 90 cm wide fabric will be cheaper, and may appear a better value, but keep in mind that having more width to work with may end up resulting in higher efficacy, saving you money and time in the end.

✿ Shopping Online

There are a limited number of craft stores carrying fabrics well suited for Cosplay. In the event that one of these stores is not positioned near you, shopping online is very convenient. Shopping online affords you less opportunity to examine the fabric before you choose to purchase it, though there are some stores that will send you samples upon request.

◆ onlinefabricstore.net

◆ fabric.com

◆ fabricdepot.com

◆ hancockfabrics.com

3-03 | How to Make Magic Girl Luncasis

We tried making the costume of this book's main character, Magic Girl Luncasis. Designing and making your own costume is one of the most exciting parts of Cosplay. Take a look through the following instructions to get an idea of the whole process.

❀ Check Over the Costume Design

First get all the materials you will need ready. Getting an official character book or figurine will help you get a handle on the design you want to make.

Then you have to think about the way the costume is composed. As an example we have made a list of the major components of Luncasis's costume below.

Her costume is mostly a one-piece dress, but here we make the skirt and top separately before joining them. The colors you use are up to you!

① Two Hair Ribbons

② Choker

③ Chest Broach

④ Chest Ribbon

⑤ Shoulder Frills

⑥ Puff Sleeves and Skirt

⑦ Double Layered Skirt

⑧ Corset

⑨ Wrist Decorations

⑩ Pink Stockings

⑪ Decorated Shoes

⑫ **The Back of the One Piece Dress is Tied**

⑬ **Large Ribbon in the Back**

⑭ **Paniers to Add Volume to the Skirt**

Luncasis is a cute design built mostly around a fluffy skirt and a variety of ribbons. Make sure to get a solid idea of the overall composition before focusing on the parts. It is important to maintain overall balance. The one-piece, corset, ribbons, choker, and shoe decorations will all be explained in detail in this chapter. The shoes will be made in the following chapter. The corset and one-piece can both be used for a maid outfit too.

🌸 Making the "Puffy-Sleeved" One-Piece Dress

Necessary materials:*

Poly/Cotton Broadcloth Blend

(one-piece top and skirt, double layers: light pink) 1.5 m

Velour (sleeve ribbons: wine-red) 50 cm

Bias Tape (choker: wine-red) 2 m

Concealed Fastener (light pink) 60 mm

Polyester Twill (shoulders and skirt: light pink) 2 m

Braided Border (skirt decorations: pink) 3 m

Lace (skirt decorations: 5cm width) 3 m

Tulle Netting (Shoulders: pink: #50) 50x50 cm

*Material measurements are estimates.

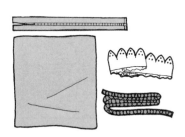

We went with a soft, cotton lace. The Tulle Netting is a relatively stiff #50. The braided border is used to run a pink line along the trim of the dress. It can be purchased at normal craft shops, along with ribbons and lace.

◆ Tools

These are the tools we used when making the costume. Chapter 4 goes into more detail.

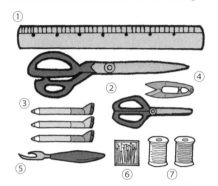

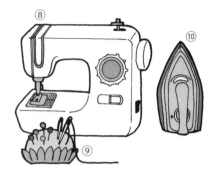

① Ruler

② Scissors (average length and large)

③ Chalk Pencil (three colors)

④ Thread Cutters

⑤ Seam Ripper

⑥ Silk Pins

⑦ Thread

⑧ Sewing Machine

⑨ Needles

⑩ Iron

◆ Instructions

1. Prepare Your Stencils and Design Guides

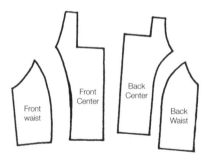

These can be downloaded and printed at the following:
http://www.ohmsha.co.jp/data/link/978-4-274-06861-4
(Download **cosplay_katagami.zip**)

2. Cut the Fabric

Fold the Broadcloth in half. Trace the stencils onto it, leaving a centimeter of extra space on each side before cutting out the designs. By folding the fabric in half, you can make both left and right portions at the same time.

3. Cut the Fabric For the Skirt

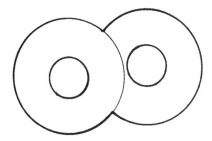

Cut the broadcloth for the skirt. This will be a double flair skirt. To produce a waist of 64 cm, the interior of the circle should be 32 cm. The first layer length (broadcloth) should be 40 cm. Make two. The second layer length (polyester) will be 30 cm. Make two. For your own waist, measure the circumference and divide by two.

4. Cut the Fabric for the Shoulders

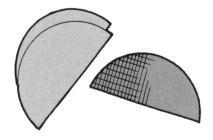

Cut the fabric (polyester) for the shoulders. The shoulders will be stuffed with Tulle Netting to help them hold their shape, so prepare Tulle Netting cuts of equal size.

5. Sew the Body of the Dress

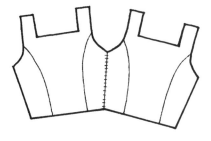

Use silk pins to pin the top of the dress together, then sew the line and iron the seam.

6. Sew the Skirt

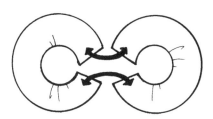

Cut the circles along the radius and attach to each other at a 720 degree angle (2 x 360). The one-piece skirt layer and the first layer. You will end up with two 720 degree circles.

7. Stack the Skirts and Sew Them

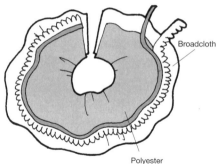

Broadcloth

Polyester

Once the circles are stacked, sew them together, attaching them with the lace and braided border. The illustration is of the skirt seen from the outside.

8. Sew the Body to the Skirt

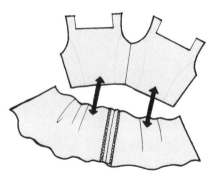

Turn the skirt inside out and sew it to the body of the dress at the waist.

9. Sew the shoulders

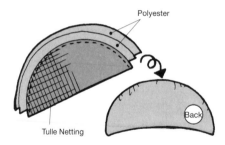

Polyester

Back

Tulle Netting

Sew the tulle to the interior of the shoulder decorations and then turn right side out.

10. Pull the Shoulders Into Shape

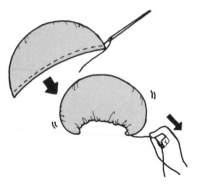

Hand sew the bottom edge of the shoulder decorations, but before tying off the thread, pull it so as to scrunch the sewn edge together. Do the same with the opposite shoulder before closing off the opening.

11. Attach the Shoulders

Sew the shoulder decorations from step ten onto the body of the dress.

12. Attach the Bias Tape

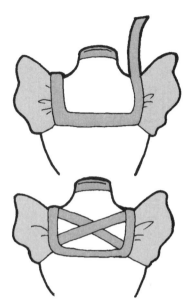

Cover the seams of the shoulders with bias tape as indicated, forming a cross over the back.

13. Cut the Sleeves

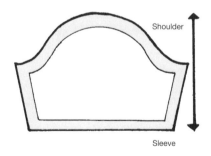

Cut the sleeves (broadcloth) to the indicated shape. The rounded area will face the shoulders, where the flat area will form the end of the sleeves.

14. Cut the Sleeve Decorations

Form the sleeve decorations from broadcloth. The frills are easily formed with a circular stencil. You will need two decorations for each sleeve.

15. Make the Sleeve Decorations

Stack the decorations on top of one another and sew the exterior edge (the ruffled edge). Cut as indicated above.

16. Turn Them Inside Out and Iron Them

After sewing the opening, turn the decorations so the sewn edge will be on the interior. Iron flat.

17. Scrunch the Sleeve Decorations

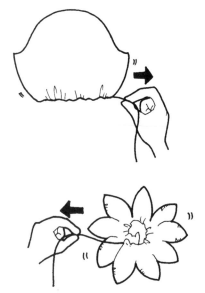

Measure your arms and then scrunch the opening of the sleeves so that they are an appropriate size. Sew the sleeve decorations to the sleeve openings, much like you did with the shoulder decorations.

18. Sew the Sleeve Ribbons

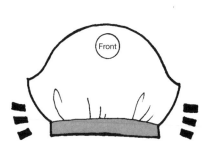

Cover the sleeve openings with wine red velour and sew them shut. Be sure that the scrunched opening lies as flat as possible when sewing.

19. Loosely Sew the Sleeve Openings

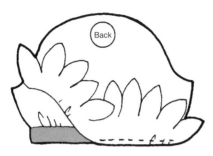

Take the scrunched side of the sleeve decorations and sew them to the velour.

20. Sew the Sleeve Decorations from the Top

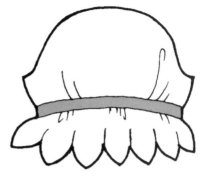

Use a sewing machine to sew the velour down, and fix the final shape.

21. Pull the Shoulder-End of the Sleeves

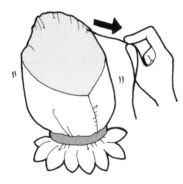

Sew the free end of the sleeve and gather the ridges together. This is the final shape of the sleeve.

22. Sew the Concealed Fastner onto the Body

Sew the concealed fastener to the sides of the dress body. Flip the dress inside out and insert the sleeves into the sleeve holes, sewing them to the body of the dress.

23. Pull the Sleeves Out

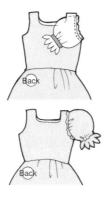

The sleeves have a front and back, so check to make sure they are positioned correctly. Then pull the sleeves out.

24. Finish the Dress

Once all the parts are attached the dress is set right side out. The panniers act to add volume to the skirt.

Making the Corset

The Corset that forms the waist of Luncasis's costume is colorful and decorative, though complex. Beginners might think it intimidating, but think of it as part of your training. It's easier than it looks!

◆ **Necessary Materials and Tools** *Material measurements are estimates.

Broadcloth Blend (same as the dress: light pink) 30x30 cm

Polyester (same as the skirt: pink) 30x30 cm

Velour (wine-red) 50 cm

Satin (red) 30 cm

Elastic (8mm) 1.5m (8 15cm strips)

Bias Tape (red) 1.5m

Zipper (wine-red, 22cm) 1 strip

Soft hooks (light pink) 10

Cotton Ribbon (light pink) 2m

Interlining (for strength) 30cm x 1m, scissors, needles

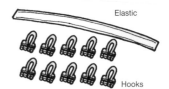

Elastic

Hooks

The zipper and hooks will be sold at craft shops. The elastic should be available at the same stores. It is sold wrapped on a spool, the same way that ribbon is. The shop staff will cut it to your requested amount. You will cut off what you need from the strip when it comes time to use it.

◆ Instructions

1. Cut Out the Parts and Sew Them

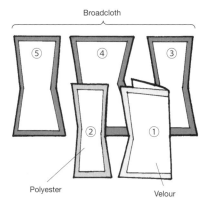

Sew the parts together so that the front and backside colors all match. The stomach and back section are surrounded on each side by three parts. Sew them with a space of 1 cm or so between each stitch.

2. Attach the Hooks

3. Sew All the Parts Together

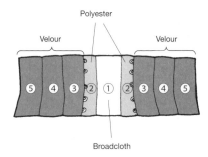

Sew the velour parts (3-5) to the stomach area. The hooks should be on the interior of the design.

4. Attach the Zipper

Attach the zipper to section 5 of the velour (where there are no hooks). Try wrapping the corset around a torso and closing the zipper to ensure it works properly before moving on.

5. Attach the Elastic

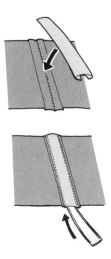

Open all the seams (there are 8) and iron flat. Cover the seams with bias tape. Insert the elastic into the Bias tape, this will ensure the shape is maintained.

6. Attach the End Covers

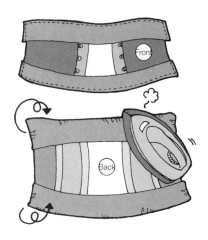

Take the satin, which has already been dyed with the interlining. Flip inside out and attach with an iron.

7. Use a Hem Stitch on the End Covers

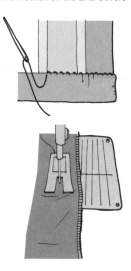

To keep the end-covers from peeling up, use a hemstitch to keep them down. When finished, use the same stitch on the exterior side of the zipper, and the final shape is finished.

8. Thread the Ribbon Through the Hooks and Finish the Corset

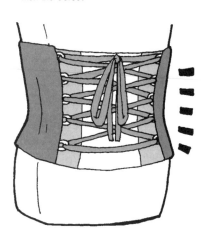

Wrap around a torso and thread ribbon through the hooks, pulling them tight and finishing with a bow.

Luncasis's costume includes two large ribbons, on the front and back. Here we will go over how to increase the volume and keep the shape intact. Once you figure out how to do it, the same techniques can be applied to other projects.

◆ **Necessary Materials and Tools** *Material measurements are estimates.

Tulle (pink: #50) 2 m

Satin (light pink) 2 m

Laundry Pins (large and small) 1 each

Snap buttons

Jewels

Scissors and Needles

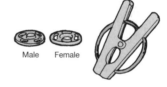

Male   Female

Snap buttons have male (protruding) and female (opening) parts.

◆ **Instructions**

We'll start with the big ribbon on the front of the costume.

1. Cut the Tulle and Satin

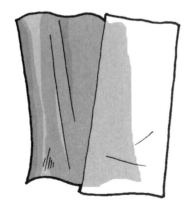

(chest ribbon: 30 x 24 cm)
(back ribbon: 52 x 38 cm)

2. Fold in Half and Sew the Longer Side

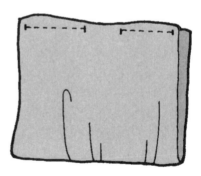

Stack the tulle and satin on one another, with the tulle on the outside. Then fold them in half. Leaving a space of 5 cm or so free in the center of the longest side, stitch the longer side at a spacing of approximately 1 cm.

3. Sew the Remaining Sides

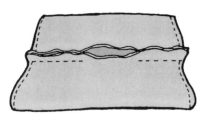

Sew both the left and right sides. Try to approximate 1 cm stitches. This is very much like making a tissue case.

4. Cut the Corners

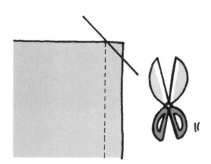

Take scissors and cut all four of the corners as close as possible to the stitching without actually cutting the stitching. Cutting these corners will improve the appearance of the ribbon when it is turned inside out.

5. Turn Inside Out and Iron

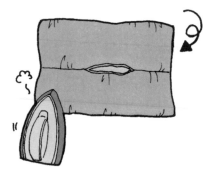

Put your finger in the opening and turn the whole thing inside out. Use a stick or small tool to push out the corners if necessary. Once everything is inside out, iron the ribbon flat. Use a low setting on the iron.

6. Form the Ribbon Shape

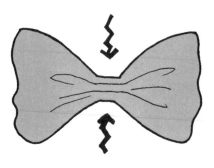

Fold the center about three times and form the shape of the ribbon.

7. Make Two Ribbons

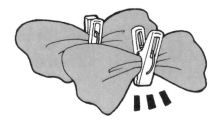

Use laundry pins to clip the folded sections of the ribbons shut.

8. Stack the Ribbons and Sew Them Together

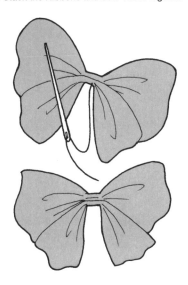

Use thick thread to make the stitching simpler. You want to sew through the stacked areas in the center.

9. Form the Center of the Ribbon and Sew it to the Ribbon Shape

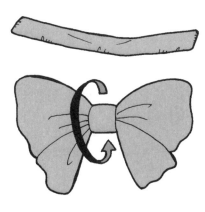

Take a 2 cm strip of satin and wrap it around the center of the ribbon, sewing it in place as shown.

10. Finish the Chest Ribbon

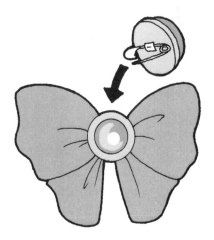

Use a safety pin to affix the jewel to the center and your ribbon is completed! The jewel can easily be obtained at any Cosplay shop or craft store.

11. Make the Back Ribbon

Now let's go onto the ribbon for the back of the costume. The process is the same as the chest ribbon through step 6. The illustration above is for the bottom section of the bow, which is the same up through step 5. The ribbon will look better if the interior sides are diagonal.

12. Finish the Back Ribbon

Just as in step 9, stack the two portions of the ribbon and sew them in the center. The back ribbon is complete.

13. Attach the Snap Buttons

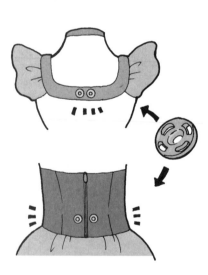

Sew the female (open hole) sides of the snap buttons onto the back of the one-piece and the corset.

14. Attach the Back Ribbon to the Dress

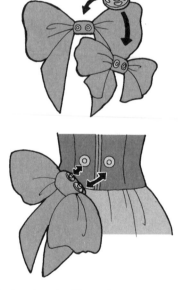

Sew the male portion of the snap buttons onto the center of the ribbon. The ribbons may also be attached by safety pin, but the addition of snap buttons makes the attachment and removal much simpler at busy events, and it is also much easier to store them and have the ribbons maintain their shape.

Making Hair and Boot Decorations

To really bring a character to life, you must pay attention to small details, like hair decorations or decorations for shoes. The decorations for Luncasis's hair and boots are the same colored ribbons. There are also flowers on her boots. Here we explain the process for making ribbons to be pushed into hair, and for making ribbons separately for the boots. If you keep the decorations as separate parts from the actual clothing, it is simpler to carry and store them.

◆ **Necessary Materials and Tools** *Material measurements are estimates.

Velvet or Velour (black) 1 m

Satin (black) 1 m

Stiff Board 1

Comb Clips (black) 2

Artificial Flowers (pink, large) 2

1 cm wide Elastic Band 60 cm

Iron, Scissors, Needles

◆ **Instructions**

1. Cut the Materials

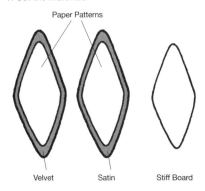

Paper Patterns

Velvet   Satin   Stiff Board

Using a paper pattern cut a shape like a leaf, cut out pieces of velvet, satin, and stiff board. The stiff board does not need any margin for sewing.

2. Attach the Stiff Board

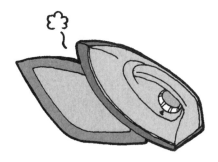

Set your iron to medium and attach the stiff board to the center of the satin leaf. The stiff board will help the ribbons to keep their shape, and prevent the other materials from stretching.

3. Line Up the Fabrics and Sew Them

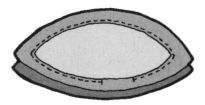

Stack the satin and velvet so that their outsides are facing one another. Sew around the perimeter, leaving 3 cm of space at the bottom.

4. Turn Inside Out

Turn inside out.

5. Stack and Form the Ribbon Shape

Make another copy of steps 1-4 and fold the centers about three times. Stack them just as with the chest ribbon.

6. Wrap the Stacked Center in Satin

Wrap the stacked centers in satin and sew them in place. The ribbons are finished!

7. Make More Ribbons

Just as you made other ribbons, make more. The ribbons for the boots should be slightly larger than those for your hair.

8. Attach the Comb Clips and Your Hair Decorations are Complete

To make attaching the hair decorations simpler, sew comb clips onto the back of the hair decorations.

9. Attach the Artificial Flowers to Your Boot Ribbons

Attach artificial flowers to the boot ribbons. If the flowers have wire attached use that to affix them, if not, sew them to the ribbons.

10. Make Black Scrunchies

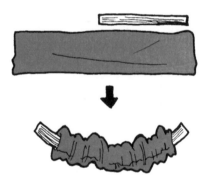

Using the satin and elastic in a ratio of 2:1 to make satin scrunchies.

11. Sew the Scrunchie to the Ribbons

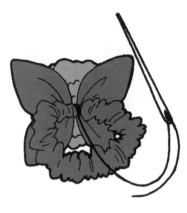

Sew the scrunchie to the ribbons to form a single piece.

12. Finish the Boot Decorations

Use the scrunchies to attach the ribbons to the boots. Now the boots can be worn plain or decorated. * We explain how to make the boots in chapter 4.

🌸 Making the Wrist Decorations

Let's go over how to make Luncasis's wristbands. The illustrations show white frills. To make them look even better we are going to use a glossy fabric. You will want to check the final design to make sure the size is properly balanced to your overall costume. That's one of the fun things about making your own clothes and props!

◆ **Necessary materials and tools** *Material measurements are estimates.

Polyester Twill (same fabric as skirt: pink) 23cm X 12cm, 2 sets

Stiff Board 21cm X 5cm, 2 sets

Velcro (light pink) 10cm

Chiffon (for the band: white) 1 m

Artificial Flowers (same as the boot

decorations: pink) 2 sets

Ribbons (see directions for hair and boot

decorations) 2

Scissors, Sewing needles

◆ Instructions

1. Cut the Fabric

We are going to make the wristbands from the same material as the skirt. Cut the fabric to the width of your wrist. Just as we did for the sleeves, you will make flowery frills. The frills will be stacked, and you will need two sets for a total of four frills.

2. Sew the Velcro

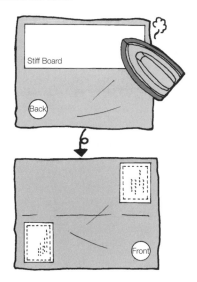

After ironing on the stiff board, cut the Velcro into two pieces and attach as shown in the above diagram.

3. Form the Frills

Just as you did for the sleeves (see page 68), form the frills. Make sure to cut the corners before turning inside out.

4. Attach the Frills to the Wristbands

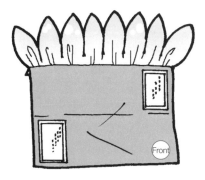

Attached the gathered frills to the wristband and sew them in place.

5. Cut the Corners and Turn Inside Out

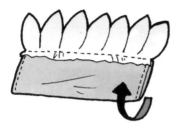

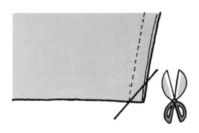

Fold the wristband in half, sew it shut, and cut the corners before turning inside out.

6. Sew the Border

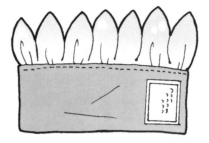

Clean up the margins. Take the left over fabric hanging over from where you sewed on the frills, and push it inside, then sew shut.

7. Sew on the Ribbon Decorations

Sew the ribbon and flower decoration onto the center of the wristband.

8. Finish the Wrist Decoration

Use the velcro to fix the wristband to your wrist. The wristband is finished!

The choker is a simple accessory for your neck, and one that can be worn with normal clothes too. Instead of just wrapping a ribbon around your neck, let's try to make a nice one, one that is a real part of the costume.

◆ **Necessary Materials and Tools** *Material measurements are estimates.

Velour (wine red) 45 cm X 7 cm

Velcro 3 cm X 1.5 cm

Scissors, sewing needles (sewing machine)

◆ **Instructions**

1. Cut the Fabric

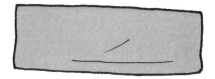

Measure the circumference of your neck. Add 2 or 3 centimeters to it and cut a rectangle of the resulting length from your fabric. Fold in half the long way and we will sew it shut.

2. Sew and Turn Inside Out

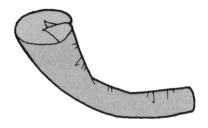

You should have a tube shaped object, turn it inside out so the seam is on the interior.

3. Attach the Velcro

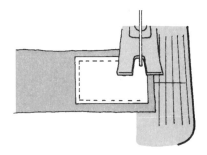

Sew the velcro to the end of the choker. You may sew by hand, but a machine will produce better results. If you sew the bristles to the side of the choker that sits against your neck, they won't scratch you during the day.

4. Finish the Choker

Use the velcro to fasten the choker and the choker is finished!

How to Take Care of Your Costume

Costumes are different from normal clothes. They have many little design details and they are not worn everyday. Because of these things, there are some special steps to be taken when washing and storing your costume. We will go over them here.

❀ How to Wash Your Costume

Costumes are typically washed by hand. If you find a stain from drink or food, be sure to wash it as quickly as possible. Fill a sink with warm water, and add a little detergent to it. Add the costume and calmly swish it through the water, rubbing trouble spots with your hands. Rinse with clean water until no detergent remains. When you are finished washing, quickly hang it out to dry in a shady area.

① Wash by Hand

Swish calmly through warm, soapy water.

② Rinse

Rinse until no detergent remains.

③ Hang in Shade

Try to hang it in the shade where there is a good breeze.

Depending on the materials you've used, you may find some easier to clean than others. For such fabrics, spray them with a deodorant and disinfectant before hanging them in the shade. There are some cleaners that specialize in cleaning costumes. If you have a costume that you really love and plan on using it for a long time, consider having it professionally cleaned.

Costumes, like normal clothes, are typically folded and shut away. When it's time to store your costume, it is a good idea to store your props with it. This is made simpler by putting them all together into a large transparent bag.

For velour, leatherette, or other materials that wrinkle easily, simply hang them and store them in your closet. If you decide to hang them in your room, try to keep them out of direct sunlight. You may consider putting them in a suit cover before hanging them.

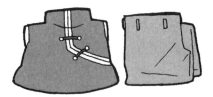

Fold Nicely and Shut Them Away.

Props are easily managed by storing them with your costume in a transparent bag. This way the bag doesn't need to be opened to check its contents.

For fabrics that wrinkle easily, hanging them in your closet is the best option.

If you decide to hang the costume in your room, consider using a suit cover.

Should You Buy a Costume or Make One?

The main thing to keep in mind when faced with this decision is your standards. You don't want to settle for anything tacky and cheap. This goes for buying a costume, or for choosing materials to make your own.

Beginners are often troubled by the question of purchasing a costume or of making their own. The answer is simple: It doesn't really matter. Making your own costume doesn't make you a better Cosplayer, nor does purchasing a costume mean that you lack passion. What is important is your desire to Cosplay, your devotion to the character, and your commitment to bringing that character to life.

However, you should avoid things that appear tacky and cheap. Reaching for a cheap costume in a pinch just because you want to Cosplay soon is something you should try hard to avoid. Tacky costumes exhibit the following:

• Thin, see-through fabric

• Shiny, floppy fabrics

• Glossy materials found at party supply shops

• Easily wrinkled

• Colors are bland, or gaudy

• Doesn't match the character (for purchased costumes)

Sometimes it is hard to tell what constitutes a cheap, tacky look. Keep your eyes open all the time, looking at normal clothes as well, and soon you will get it.

An easy and simple way to start Cosplaying, like I did, is to pick a character that doesn't need a lot of costume alterations. If you are already dead-set on a complicated character costume, consider asking a person or shop your trust to help you make the main costume, giving you time to work on the details by yourself. You may not get it all perfect the first time, but always try to do better than just making "something to wear." Cosplaying is more fun that way!

Chapter 4

Preparing Your Props

❶ Using Pre-Existing Objects

❷ Prop-Making and Common Materials

❸ How to Improve Shoes

❹ Making Magic Girl Luncasis's Boots

COLUMN Convenient Materials and Tools for Prop-Making

Cosplaying uses a lot of props, from shoes and accessories to weapons. This chapter will focus on making shoes, while introducing the basics of prop making.

I THINK WE SHOULD TRY MAKING ALTERATIONS TO A PAIR OF PURCHASED BOOTS. THAT'S WHAT WE NORMALLY DO.

OH YEAH?

SO YOU JUST MAKE WHATEVER PROPS AREN'T AVAILABLE FOR SALE?

YOU BET!

COSPLAYING IS POPULAR ENOUGH THAT YOU CAN FIND A LOT OF ACCESSORIES AND PROPS AND WEAPONS FOR SALE,

BUT WHATEVER YOU CAN'T FIND, JUST MAKE IT FROM SCRATCH!

NEKOMIMI ACCESSORY

ヘえ〜! YOU DON'T SAY...

WOW, COOL!

BUT IT SOUNDS HARD...

IT'S FINE, YOU CAN BUY ALL THE THINGS YOU NEED, AND JUST WORK ON IT A LITTLE AT A TIME!

うん...! れっ!

Toy the

おもちゃの トイ

SALE

CRAFTS 手芸

TOOLS 工具

WOW, THERE'S SO MUCH WE COULD USE FOR COSPLAYING!

I KNOW! IT'S PARADISE! IT REALLY IS! まさに!!

YAY さく

YAY さく

THEY SELL TONS OF STUFF YOU CAN USE TO MAKE PROPS AND ACCESSORIES.

LIKE WHAT?

LIKE THIS LION BOARD RIGHT HERE!

ライオンボード

YOU CAN CUT AND BEND IT EASILY, SO ITS GREAT FOR MAKING SHIELDS AND ARMOR.

YOU CAN MAKE ARMOR OUT OF THIS? WOW...

BOING ばよ

BOING ばよ

PEOPLE ALSO USE STYROFOAM A LOT.

NORMALLY YOU CUT OR SHAVE THEM INTO THE SHAPE YOU WANT BEFORE GLUING THE PIECES TOGETHER.

LIKE A WORKSHOP, OR MODELING?

TO MAKE METALLIC OBJECTS, LIKE ARMOR, YOU JUST COVER THE EXTERIOR IN A METALLIC, SHINY FABRIC.

SPARKLE

SPARKLE

いろんな色があるよ

THERE ARE TONS OF COLORS!

ALL THE DIFFERENT MATERIALS HAVE THEIR OWN SPECIALTIES AND ISSUES. YOU'LL GET THE HANG OF IT!

I'LL TRY!

TODAY LET'S FOCUS ON GETTING WHAT YOU NEED FOR THE BOOTS!

工具

あっちのコーナーだね
RIGHT OVER THERE!

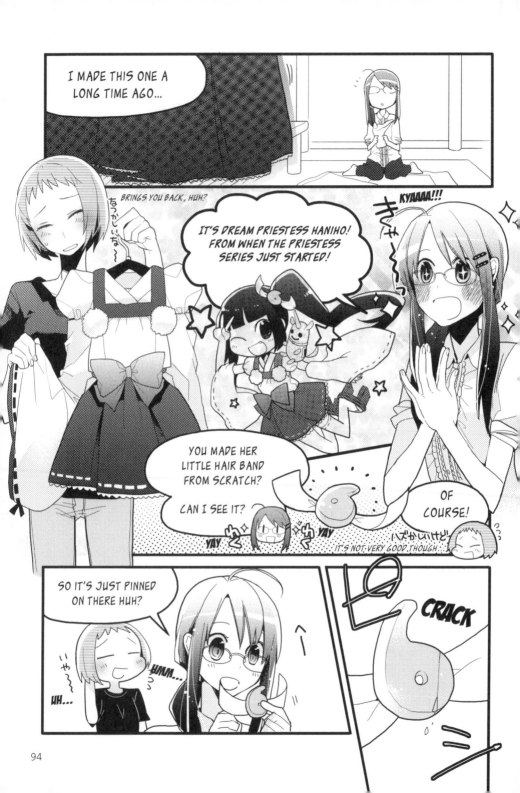

I MADE THIS ONE A LONG TIME AGO...

BRINGS YOU BACK, HUH?

IT'S DREAM PRIESTESS HANIHO! FROM WHEN THE PRIESTESS SERIES JUST STARTED!

KYAAAA!!!

YOU MADE HER LITTLE HAIR BAND FROM SCRATCH?

CAN I SEE IT?

OF COURSE!

YAY

YAY

IT'S NOT VERY GOOD, THOUGH...

SO IT'S JUST PINNED ON THERE HUH?

HMM...

UH...

CRACK

4−01 | Using Pre-Existing Products

There are a lot of anime and game character props being sold as toys that can be used just as they are for Cosplaying. Pay attention to size and quality when you look for the perfect props.

✿ Buying Toys

Often times you can find toys being sold that represent the character you are going to Cosplay. These are designed as toys for children, so occasionally they are small and manufactured poorly, but there are many that will work perfectly for Cosplaying. Make sure you can see the toy in person to check its size and quality before purchasing.

Character animal companions are often sold as stuffed animals, and they can easily be found in many toy stores.

✿ Buying at a Speciality Store

Among Cosplay clubs and Cosplay specialty stores, there are people that sell props. Specialty stores often carry very high-quality and rare items, but they can be very expensive, even over-priced. Make sure you feel that the balance between price and quality is worth it before purchasing.

Often when you find just the piece you are looking for there will be only one left, or the item will be on back-order, so be sure to ask about availability.

Prop-Making and Common Materials

There is some molding involved in making props. Try various means of production and materials as you progress and slowly improve your skills. Here we introduce the most common materials and their attributes.

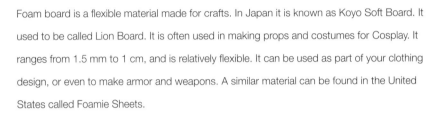

✿ Foam Board

Foam board is a flexible material made for crafts. In Japan it is known as Koyo Soft Board. It used to be called Lion Board. It is often used in making props and costumes for Cosplay. It ranges from 1.5 mm to 1 cm, and is relatively flexible. It can be used as part of your clothing design, or even to make armor and weapons. A similar material can be found in the United States called Foamie Sheets.

1. Create the Model

When making props from foam board, first use a thick card stock and tape to make a model shape of the final prop. This model will end up being the exact same measurements as the final prop, so make sure you make it as well as you can. Next, these shapes will be placed on the foam board and traced. The parts will be cut out and assembled with bonding glue.

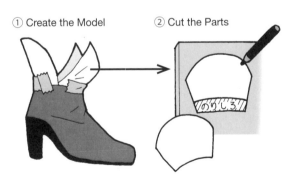

① Create the Model
② Cut the Parts
③ Put it Together

Using card stock and tape, create the shape you want the prop to be in the end. These will become the final pattern, so keep working at it until you get it just right.

Unfold the card stock and place it on the foam board, using a marker to trace its outline. Then cut out the parts.

Glue the foam board parts together with bonding glue. Curved surfaces can be formed with darts (interior cuts) and can be set in place with the glue.

2. Form the Surface

For making armor and costume parts, a simple process that is often used in the Cosplay community is applying leatherette to the surface of the foam board. This can often produce better results than painting.

There are very glossy leatherettes and we recommend these. If you chose stretchable two-way enamel leatherette, you can make curved surfaces look smooth.

Use adhesive to attach the leatherette to the surface of the foam board. First cut the leatherette to a size slightly larger than you will need. Paint the pre-cut foam board with adhesive, and then let it dry for ten minutes or so before laying it onto the leatherette.

① Cut the Leatherette   ② Paint the Adhesive   ③ Attach the Leatherette

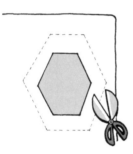  

Cut the leatherette larger than necessary, so that it completely covers the foam board parts.

Paint the pre-cut foam board parts with adhesive and allow it to dry for ten minutes.

Lay the leatherette over the surface of the foam board and press to adhere.

When you have multiple parts to be assembled, you should assemble the foam board parts before attaching the leatherette surface. Try to stretch the leatherette a bit when you apply it to the adhesive. In areas that look tight, apply a little heat to the surface and that area will stretch more. Try to avoid wrinkling the surface or allowing air bubbles to form.

> When making props, be careful! Avoid burns or accidents. When working with adhesives or solvents, make sure there is enough ventilation in the room!

❋ Styrofoam

Styrofoam is easy to procure and easy to work with as it can be cut very easily. It is a very convenient material. You can buy it at any home improvement center. Styrofoam is very light and so it is great for making large props like weapons.

If you paint the surface directly, there is a chance it may melt. Before painting, cover the surface in working glue or gesso for oil painting. This will make the process much simpler and the outcome superior.

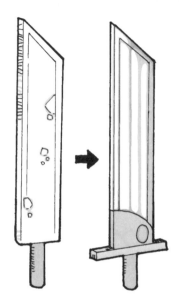

When making large weapons from Styrofoam, you should add a stiffener insert, as it strengthens the final product. PVC piping is great for this!

❋ Clay and Crystal Resin

Paper mache, resin clays, and oven clays are available. You can mix wood glue into paper mache to increase its durability, but resin and oven clays are more durable in the long run. Oven clay won't harden until it is baked, which makes it very easy to work with.

To make clear props or jewelry, crystal resin can be used. To do so, you make a mold from silicone, pour in the resin, and let it harden. Typically it is clear, but can easily be colored with readily available colorings. It is a comparatively advanced material.

4−03 | How to Improve Shoes

Depending on the costume, you may be able to just use normal, commercial available shoes. However, the time will come for original designs. When your desired design is not available for purchase, you can try and make it by modifying available shoes.

Choosing the Shoes

When purchasing shoes to modify, look for the simplest shoes you can find. Finding a shoe that shares characteristics with the desired final design will make it easier to achieve the result you want.

Buying thick-soled shoes will make you taller and may help with your overall design, depending on the character. When Cosplaying a character in a school-uniform, the typical uniform loafers are probably available for purchase.

Changing Shoe Color

When the color shoe you want isn't available, you can change the color by dying them, or by using fabric to cover their exterior.

The easiest way to dye shoes is to use a spray dye. Certain spray dyes can also be used to paint color onto vinyl shoes.

Covering the exterior in fabric is often done using velour or leatherette. The trick is to attach the fabric in such a way that the seams will not be visible. For larger design changes, use foam board to make additions.

4−04 Making Magic Girl Luncasis's Boots

Magic Girl Luncasis's boots can be made by making simple modifications to commercially available boots. Take a look at the directions to get a feel for the process and design.

✽ Check the Design

Luncasis's boots are split down the center, and have some interesting design elements.

① Front and Back Parts

② Black Ribbon and Flowers

③ The Boot Color is White

④ Heels and Sides are Red

The color of the boots will be created by attaching leatherette to the exterior. The unnecessary parts will be trimmed and used elsewhere, so you need not worry about the length of the boots. Designing custom shoes and boots is difficult to do from scratch, but adding design elements to pre-existing shoes is relatively simple. In this case, we will take the heels and bottom of the shoes from some longer boots that seem to match the design. Then we will add design elements and change the color.

✽ Necessary Materials and Tools

The following materials and tools will be needed to make Luncasis's boots. Scissors and utility knives can be purchased at any craft or home improvement center.

◆ Necessary Materials and Tools*

1 pair of long boots

Styrofoam board, 3mm thick letter size

Leatherette (enamel stretch: white) 1 m

Leatherette (for heels and sides: red) 50 cm x 50 cm

Boot decorations, 2 (see chapter 3)

Paper card stock (for the patterns)

Utility knife, cutting matt, scissors, tape, spray primer, and instant dry adhesive.

*Material measurements are estimates

When the utility knife stops cutting well, break off the end of the blade. The excess blades can be disposed of in the blade disposal box. Maintenance should not be limited to your utility knife, take care of all your tools with periodic maintenance checks.

❀ Instructions

1. Draw the Guidelines

Because you purchased long boots, some of the tall section will be unnecessary. Comparing the shoes to a character model, draw a guideline of where you think the tops should be cut off. You will later cut along this line.

2. Cut Off Unnecessary Parts

When you cut the boots, make sure the zipper is unzipped all the way. If you cut them with the zipper zipped all the way up, you will not be able to reattach the zipper pull.

3. Create the Backing

The brim of the shoe flairs out in the front and back. Using card stock and tape, attempt to recreate the shape of these brims. Keep trying until you get it just right. The final shape will be made from foam board, so don't worry if you get tape all over everything at this stage.

4. Create the Tongue

Just as you did with the back brim, create the design of the flared tongue using card stock and tape.

5. Remove Patterns

Cut off the card stock patterns.

6. Trace Patterns Onto Foam Board

Place the card stock patterns on the foam board and trace them carefully with a marker. Add an additional centimeter at the bottom to use as a gluing area.

7. Cut the Parts Out

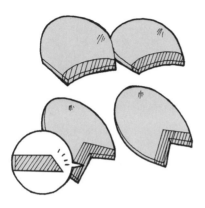

Use a utility knife to cut out the pattern you've traced onto the foam board. To make gluing easier later, cut a bevel into the additional centimeter you left on the bottom in the previous step.

8. Glue the Parts to the Shoe

Put instant dry adhesive onto the surface of the shoe and the foam board. Allow it to dry for 10 minutes before applying it to the interior of the shoe. Apply pressure with your fingertips until the adhesive has set.

9. Prepare the Patterns for the Leatherette

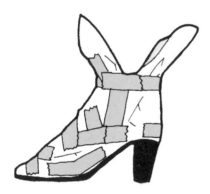

Prepare to cover the shoe with leatherette. Cut a large quantity of paper and use tape to cover the entire surface of the shoe, including the brims, with the paper.

10. Remove the Card Stock Patterns

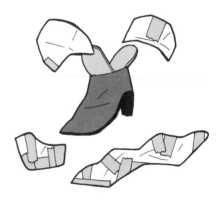

Remove the paper and cut it into pieces. This time, because the center portion curves and is difficult to reproduce, we have cut that portion into halves. Because the center of the shoe is easily visible, it is better to try and design your cuts so that the seams fall on the sides or back. However, because cutting the center is easier, we have chosen to go that route this time.

11. Cut the Leatherette

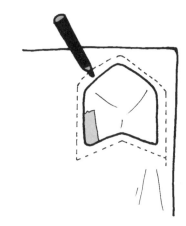

Take your card stock patterns and trace them onto the leatherette. When you cut the leatherette, cut it slightly larger than necessary to give yourself some wiggle room.

12. Glue the Leatherette to the Shoe

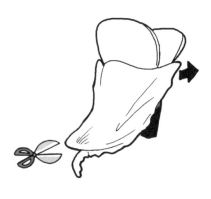

Apply instant dry adhesive to the leatherette and shoes. Allow it to dry for 10 minutes. When you apply the leatherette to the shoes, take special care around the curve on the front, carefully following its curve with the leatherette. Remove excess leatherette with scissors.

13. Glue the Leatherette to the Heel and Sides

Glue red leatherette to the heels and sides of the shoes. If you glue anything to the actual sole of the shoe, it will be slippery and dangerous, therefore we will not attempt to color the soles here.

14. Magic Girl Luncasis's Shoes are Complete!

Convenient Materials and Tools for Prop-Making

The tools and materials necessary for prop-making can be found for approximately the prices listed below. Look for them at home improvement centers, online shops, craft shops, stationary stores, and dollar stores.

LIST	PRICE
Scissors	$1.00 to 10.00
Utility Knife	$1.00 to 10.00
Cutting Matt	$1.00 to 15.00
Masking Tape	$1.00 to 10.00
Fast Drying Adhesive	$10.00
Instant Drying Spray Primer	$10.00 to 20.00
Painting Primer	$1.00 to 15.00
Dye for Vinyl	$10.00 to $15.00
Spray Dye	$10.00
Styrofoam Board	$3.00 to $10.00
Leatherette	$7.00 and up
Velour	$5.00 to $10.00
Oven Clay	$2.00 and up
Polymer Clay	$2.00 and up

There are many different brands available and brands vary greatly between what is offered in Japan to what is offered elsewhere. So do your research and make sure you are working with quality brands for all the different construction materials listed above.

Chapter 5

Hair and Makeup

❶ Makeup Basics
❷ Using Wigs
❸ Color Contacts
❹ Details
COLUMN Hiding Your Breasts

Hair and Makeup are a big part of Cosplaying. In this chapter we will go over makeup basics, using a wig, and how to manage your appearance.

We will also go over some of our advice regarding color contacts, body paint, and underwear.

THAT IS ONE NICE LOOKING COSTUME!

HEHE えへへ〜

WHAT?

いい II

→STARE

YOU'RE EVEN GOOD AT MAKEUP... MUST BE CAUSE YOU ARE SO PRETTY...

元がイイからかな…

WHAT? NOT AT ALL!

YOU HAVE TO PUT ON MAKEUP WHEN YOU COSPLAY, RIGHT?

OF COURSE, IT'S A BIG PART OF COSPLAYING!

これ見て
TAKE A LOOK.

A MAGAZINE?

雑誌?

MEN ALSO WEAR MAKEUP?

その人も
じてるでしょ?
YOU KNOW HIM RIGHT?

YEAH! RIGHT!

WHAT'S SO DIFFERENT FROM NORMAL MAKEUP?

THE MOST IMPORTANT THING IS DAILY SKIN CARE!

I TRY TO WATCH WHAT I EAT AND HOW MUCH SLEEP I GET. I TRY TO USE A NICE LOTION TOO!

WELL A LOT OF IT IS THE SAME, BUT SOME STUFF IS DIFFERENT!

I'VE BEEN WORKING ON MY COSTUME SO MUCH THAT I PROBABLY COULD USE SOME MORE SLEEP.

THE MAIN DIFFERENCE IS HOW THICK YOU APPLY THE MAKEUP.

OF COURSE IT DEPENDS ON THE CHARACTER, BUT GOING A LITTLE HEAVY ON THE MAKEUP CAN REALLY HELP BRING A CHARACTER TO LIFE, AND DRAW ATTENTION TO YOUR COSTUME!

DEEP...

DO YOU NEED ANY SPECIAL MAKEUP?

STAGE MAKEUP CAN BE EASIER TO MATCH WITH A COSTUME.

BUT NORMAL MAKEUP IS JUST FINE!

YOU CAN USE CONCEALER AND FOUNDATION TO COVER UP PIMPLE SCARS OR MOLES OR WRINKLES!

STAGE MAKEUP IS THICKER, AND COVERS OVER BLEMISHES BETTER!

IT SEEMS LIKE YOU'D HAVE TO SPEND ALL DAY TOUCHING IT UP.

DON'T FORGET THAT YOUR WIG WILL HAVE A BIG IMPACT ON HOW THE MAKEUP LOOKS, SO MAKE SURE YOU TRY THEM OUT TOGETHER AT LEAST ONCE BEFORE THE DAY OF THE EVENT.

WHAT'S A WIG, EXACTLY?

あっ

AH! WE HAVEN'T GOTTEN YOU A WIG YET!

A WIG IS, OF COURSE, FAKE HAIR THAT SITS ON YOUR HEAD!

へぇ...!

EHHH!

I THOUGHT EVERYONE WAS DYING THEIR HAIR!

MOST OF THE TIME, YOU CAN GET CLOSER TO YOUR CHOSEN CHARACTER WITH A WIG. IT CAN BE REALLY HARD TO STYLE YOUR OWN HAIR TO MATCH.

I GUESS YOU'RE RIGHT. IT WOULD BE TOUGH TO GET THAT HAIR COLOR AND STYLE WITHOUT A WIG.

これはこの前の
冬コミの時のだよ
THIS IS FROM MY LAST EVENT.

WHAT A CUTE COSTUME!
これ可愛かった～

DIFFERENT COMPANIES HAVE DIFFERENT SIZES FOR THEIR WIGS, SO BE CAREFUL WHEN YOU BUY ONE!

THE DIFFERENT MAKERS ALL USE DIFFERENT MEASUREMENTS, AND MOST OF THE TIME YOU CAN'T RETURN A WIG!

WOOSH
ビュッ

OH NO! えーん

DUDUM

DOES IT MATTER IF THE WIG DOESN'T FIT PERFECTLY?

ずず...

あぃ あぃ

WELL IT DEPENDS ON THE STORE...

111

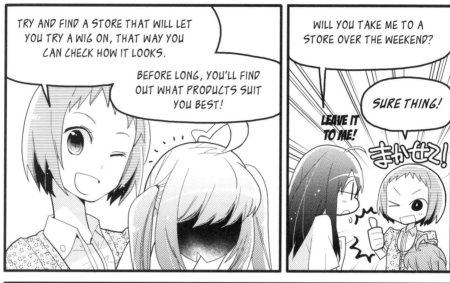

REMEMBER, THE CONTACTS GO DIRECTLY ON YOUR EYE, SO MAKE SURE THEY STAY CLEAN, READ UP ON HOW TO STORE THEM PROPERLY!

IN!

OKAY!

YOU REALLY KNOW A LOT ABOUT COSPLAYING, RIKO! I'M LEARNING SO MUCH!

すごく勉強になるよ！

WELL I LIKE IT, AND I'VE BEEN DOING IT FOR A WHILE.

え〜〜

PRETTY SOON I'LL MAKE MY BIG DEBUT!

WHAT WAS YOUR FIRST COSTUME, RIKO?

HAHA

DREAM PRIESTESS HANIHO!

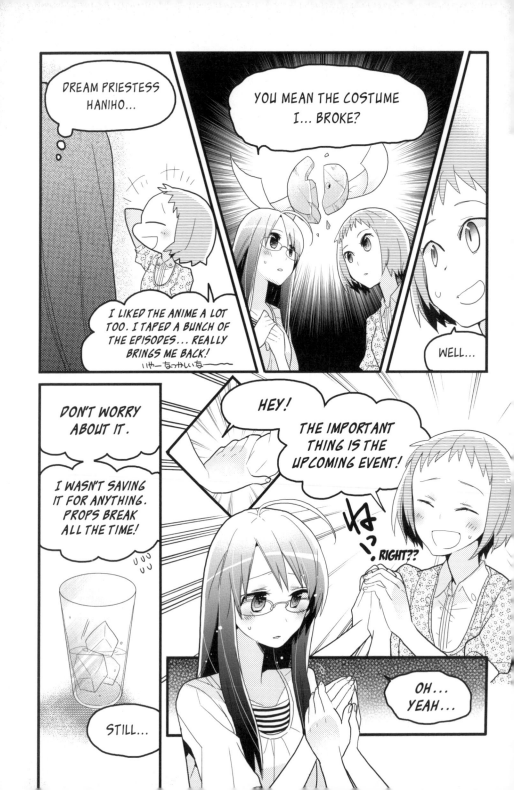

5-01 | Makeup Basics

Cosplay makeup is different than normal makeup, rather than attempting to be matt, and natural, you want to show it off. Even if you are not the type to typically use makeup, it's best to practice to prepare for an event.

✿ Preparing for Makeup

The most important things to keep in mind when preparing for the use of makeup are your daily skin care and the removal of fine hairs. Especially important is your daily skin care routine, as it will have a big impact on your skin condition. Try to eat healthy and get plenty of sleep. For daily skin care, you basically focus on washing your face and on moisturizing. After you have washed your face, make sure to use a moisturizer on your skin. If you still feel like your skin is dry, there are other creams that can be applied to help your skin retain moisture. You do not need to use expensive products. Focus on finding a product that you like.

Finally, many people forget to take care of the fine hairs on their face. These hairs will interact with the makeup, and may end up showing in photographs. Before an event, double-check the area under your nose and around your chin. Electric face shavers are convenient for touching up your eyebrows. Speaking of eyebrows, its best to pluck them thin, that way you can draw on them to match them to any character!

Daily Care is Important!

| Eat Healthy | Take Care of Your Skin | Get Plenty of Sleep |

1. The Whole Face

① First, apply face wash, moisturizer, lotion, cream, and sunblock in that order. Then follow with a thin coat of liquid makeup.

② Now apply foundation evenly to your whole face. Liquid and cream varieties are easy to use. Try and choose one that closely matches the color of your skin. Finish with powder foundation for a porcelain-like finish.

There are shops that sell makeup and tools for the stage. They are thicker than normal makeups and can cover up a man's shaving. Because of their strength, they are taxing on the skin, and are best avoided for daily use. They work great for Cosplaying though!

If you are worried about spots on your skin, a little concealer will help to hide them

③ To give more depth to your face, apply some nose shadow.

Nose shadow can be a specialty product, or can be done with brown or gray eye shadow. It is applied from the interior points of your eyebrows down the sides of the bridge of your nose. Follow the shadow application with highlight application, in a lighter color, to your 1) T-zone, 2) under your eyes, and 3) under your chin. This is best done lightly, with your fingers.

Nose Shadow

Highlights

2. Eyebrows

Eyebrows are very important, they can really draw attention to a design. Because you want to match them to your desired character, it is best to shave them very thin before hand.

Use a pencil to draw a guideline and follow it with a powder application.

You should aim to achieve balance with the color of your eyebrows and hair. So if your character has blond hair, use a light brown for your eyebrows.

When you are using single colored wigs, use a color

High Point   End
Start

The Start of the eyebrow is directly above the inside corner of the eye. The High Point is 2/3 from the Start. And the End is in direct line with the outside corner of your eye and the end of your nose.

that is just a shade or two lighter than the wig color to achieve a natural look.

If they don't sell eyebrow powder in the color of your wig, you can mix lipstick or eyeshadow into liquid foundation and use that. Apply it with the end of a cotton swab. You may also consider using a colored pencil that is close to the color of your wig. There are commercially available pencils for this purpose.

3. Eyeshadow (eyelids)

Because anime characters are 2-dimentional and have large eyes, it is best to use your eye makeup to give that impression.

First use eyeshadow to go all around the eye, as this will make the eye "pop."

Eyeshadow is typically sold in a three-color set of "base color" (bright), "main color" (middle color), and "dark color" (dark).

The base color goes all around the eyeball.

The main color goes on the bottom half of your upper eyelid.

The dark color goes right along the line of your eyelashes.

Point color (we recommend pearl) goes in a spot in the center of the eyelid.

4. Eyeliner

Use eyeliner to draw attention to the outline of your eye.

Apply eyeliner to the thickness of your eyelid, where the eyelashes grow. Applying to the bottom eyelid will make your eyes even more dramatic. Liquid eyeliner gives a stronger impression.

Apply eyeliner here.

The way you draw this line will change the overall impression of your character, so try to draw it in a way that matches the impression you are going for. Adding a double line in the indicated areas will emphasis your upper eyelid crease.

Apply double line here.

5. Eyelashes (and artificial eyelashes)

The longer you make your eyelashes look, the bigger your eyes will appear. Use an eyelash curler at the roots of the eyelashes, and then apply mascara. Use a waterproof mascara that is water and sweat resistant.

Artificial eyelashes are almost essential for Cosplaying. First apply mascara and curl your eyelashes. Then apply the artificial eyelashes. Applying mascara to your bottom eyelashes will make your eyes look even more dramatic.

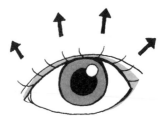

Mascara will make your eyes seem larger.

6. Cheeks and Chin

Adding blush to your cheeks will make your face look flush and healthy. Chose a color that matches the feeling of your character.

Apply the blush in an upward, diagonal line from your cheekbones, as this will give your face a sharp, defined look. Pink circles applied lightly to the center of your cheeks will make you look young, and cute, perfect for young characters.

7. Lips

Applying a layer of lip gloss over your original layer of lipstick will give your lips a moist, clear look. A thin layer will look natural, too much will make you look shiny and sticky.

Wigs and Makeup

Often times, when Cosplaying, a wig will be necessary to properly represent the character. When wearing a wig, the short hair by your temples may be visible and stand out. If it looks like this hair will be visible, put some tape or wax over it and cover with foundation.

A wig will dramatically change the way your character looks. Before the event, make sure you try your makeup routine with the wig on. The practice will make everything go more smoothly on event day.

Makeup Touch-Ups

Makeup always needs touchups during an event. Bring the following things along with you so that you can touchup your makeup when you have a break.

◆ Tissues   ◆ Cotton Swabs
◆ Face Blotting Paper   ◆ Small Mirror
◆ Foundation (powder)   ◆ Lipstick and Gloss
◆ Eyelash Glue

During the day, you want to always check to make sure your foundation is in place and that the area under your eyes has not turned black. Eye makeup, especially, stands out when it is not just right. If your mascara has run and given you dark spots under your eyes, remove it with a cotton swab.

If your foundation starts to come off, use oil-removing paper to remove the rough patch and go over it with powder.

5-02 | Using Wigs

To really bring the wild hairstyles of characters to life, a wig is probably necessary. Let's take a few minutes to learn as much as we can about them!

What is a Wig?

There are hard wigs and stretchable wigs. We prefer to use the stretchable kind. There are all kinds of wigs these days, even kinds that can easily be styled like real hair. There are even wigs made just for Cosplaying. Wigs can be found at party supply shops, but for better quality, go to a specialist. The following websites carry wigs:

◆ epiccosplay.com

◆ dolluxe.com

◆ arda-wigs.com

◆ hellocosplay.com

◆ lightinthebox.com

◆ cosplaybuzz.com

◆ matchwigs.com

What to Watch Out for When Purchasing a Wig

The first thing to be aware of when shopping for a wig, is that while the listed sizes may be identical, depending on the maker the wigs will fit differently. And because wigs purchased online cannot typically be returned, the size is a legitimate concern. If possible, you will want to visit an actual store and try on a few wigs to get an idea for the sizing.

It is important to have proper measurements for the size of your head. You do not measure your head by the circumference. The proper way to measure your

Correct measurement area

Incorrect measurement area

head for wig sizing is a line that runs diagonally over the temple and behind the ear, as shown in the illustration. Typical sizes are around 58 cm. Use this as an estimate to help you.

Wig shops often display their wigs on mannequins, but because mannequin heads are typically smaller than actual human heads, the wig may appear longer than it actually is. This means it will look shorter when you wear the wig. Be sure to be aware of this when shopping!

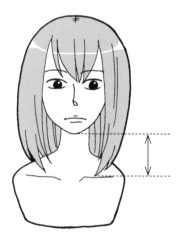

In the mannequin picture, the hair reaches down to the collarbone, appearing quite long.

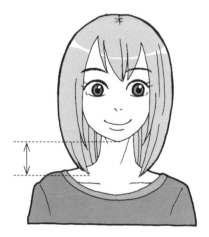

Wearing the wig in real life, the hair only reaches down to the shoulders. This appears much shorter than the wig appeared on the mannequin.

❋ How to Chose a Wig

Watch out for the following things when choosing a wig:

◆ Does the Size Match Your Head?

The most important thing is whether or not the wig will fit on your head. As we have already said, the sizes vary by maker, so the only way to be sure is to try. Find the producer that works best for you.

◆ Hair Style

There are hairstyles that are an integral part of the character, and there are also hairstyles that are simple and everyday designs. They may even sell wigs made just for the character you are Cosplaying! Regardless, choose a wig that can easily be altered to match the character's hairstyle you are aiming for.

◆ Materials

There are wigs made from real hair, as well as artificial wigs. Artificial wigs tend to be dangerous around open flames and heat, but there are some made now that are fireproof. These durable artificial wigs are simple and economical, making them great for the beginner.

◆ Color

Ironically, choosing a wig that is the exact color of the character's hair may result in a final design that seems unnatural. Very bright colors really stand out among natural materials, and therefore you may want to consider stepping down the color a bit from the way it actually appears in the character design.

Even wigs that are made specifically for Cosplaying a character are often made in slightly less-intense tones than the actual character's hair. So, if the character has bright blonde hair, the wig might be close to a dirty blonde, with some brown mixed into it, as these more relaxed colors appear more natural when worn.

❀ How to Wear a Wig

After you purchase a wig, be sure to try it on before the day of the event. You will want to double check the size and appearance before you exhibit it.

If you are not used to wearing wigs, you will want to try it on a few times, as practice, before the event.

① Tie Your Hair Up

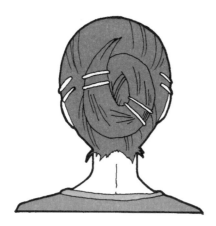

To prevent your hair from puffing up under the wig, you will want to pin down your hair using hairpins. If you have long hair, you should tie it up on the back of your head and clip it down as shown.

② Pull the Wig Net Down to Your Neck

When you buy a wig, it will come with a wig net (though occasionally these are sold separately). The elastic side would face down, and you pull it over your head and down to your neck.

③ Raise the Wig Net

Raise the wig net, taking care that it collects your hair around your temples. Once it is all collected, use a hairpin to close the top and pin it down.

④ Put the Wig on from the Front

Wigs are like brimmed hats, in that if you wear them properly they will not slip or move. Hold the wig even and slip your bangs under the front lip before pulling it all towards the back of your head and down in the back. Center the wig where your bangs would be and hold there while using your other hand to fix the back. It should wrap around the back of your head.

⑤ Pull it Down Deep

Pull the wig down so it fits snuggly.

⑥ Brush It

Use hairpins to fix the wig in place. Use a hairbrush to set the wig and make it look natural.

✿ How to Style a Wig

Most wigs are manufactured with long bangs, and therefore to match your character well, you may have to do some styling. Wigs designed for specific characters will not need this step, making them convenient.

The basic flow is brushing, cutting, and styling. Let's try our hand at it!

◆ Brushing

Wigs get tangled much more easily than real hair and therefore they must be brushed before and after use. When working with a wig, a wig stand will make your life easier. If you don't have one, use one hand to support the wig from the inside while you style it with the other hand.

① Spray the Whole Wig

Spray the wig with silicone hair spray or special wig spray and then run your fingers through the knots.

② Brush

Slowly brush the wig from tips to roots.

③ Finish

Work your way up to the roots and the brushing is finished.

Use a metal comb or a wig comb. Metal combs will not build up static electricity.

Wig Stand

Wig Brush

◆ Cut

Wig haircuts are just like people haircuts, they can be easy or difficult depending on the style. If you are going to do the cutting on your own, cut less than you originally think you need to, as once you cut too much, you can't go back.

Normal scissors will work fine, but hair cutting scissors are preferable. You can purchase them at a drugstore. They may also be sold at wig shops, in which case you can purchase them at the same time as your wig. Aside from scissors, you may use razors and face shavers as well.

Razor

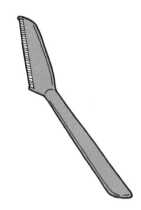

Face Shaver

We recommend using a Styrofoam wig stand when cutting your wig. Because the stand is made from Styrofoam, you can use needles and pins to hold the wig in place while you work on it.

Wig stands are normally smaller than people's heads. Take notice of this when you decide the length of the cut. Use a pen to mark the position of your eyes on the Styrofoam, and use them as a guide when you are cutting the hair.

Use a pen or magic marker to mark the position of your eyes.

① Gather the Hair into Sections

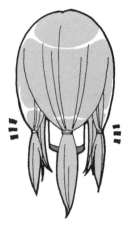

When the wig is longer than you would like, gather it into sections and pin them in place to make it easier to tell where and how much you want to cut.

② Cut the Inside Hair First

Take the outer hair and pin it up out of the way before you cut the interior hair. Hold your scissors vertically when making cuts. Using the length of the interior hair as a guide to cut the outer hair as well.

③ Cut the Hair to the Left and Right of the Bangs

Cut the hair that hangs behind your temples just as you did the rest. This hair is immediately noticeable, so be careful when deciding on a length. It will look longer on the wig stand than it will on you.

④ Cut the Bangs and Sides

Decide what part of the bangs will be longest and cut it first. Use that portion as a guide to cut the rest. When cutting the sides and bangs, you may want to put the wig on before you make the cuts. This will result in fewer mistakes.

◆ Styling

Styling wigs can be done with the same hairsprays and waxes that you use on normal hair. If you want to add cowlicks or waves to your wig, make sure that it is made from something heat-resistant. Straight and curling irons can be used on a low setting. Event changing rooms often prohibit the use of hair sprays, so when styling at an event, try to use hard waxes. Keep in mind that non-heat-resistant wigs are very dangerous around any type of heat, so don't get them anywhere near a hairdryer. We will use a common anime hairstyle as a guide here. Hair that stands up in the back!

This is a hairstyle that stands up in the back.

① **Backcomb the Hair**

Use a comb and your hands to back comb the hair in the back. To make it really stand up comb it down adjacent to itself with a fair amount of vigor. Hold the hair up and comb down from the tips to the roots.

② **Fix in Place with Wax**

Add wax to your fingertips and apply it from the roots in bunches to fix the hair in place. Spin the tips to make them sharp.

③ Use Hairspray to Fix the Design

Spray the whole wig with hairspray to keep the style in place.

Extra Techniques!

You can use clip-pin pigtails and buns to quickly rearrange any hairstyle.

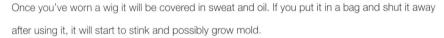

✿ How to Treat Your Wig

Once you've worn a wig it will be covered in sweat and oil. If you put it in a bag and shut it away after using it, it will start to stink and possibly grow mold.

After you have worn a wig, don't store it right away, but let it sit in the sun for a day or so. If you use a hollow, open wig stand then you can just sit the wig on that.

After you have worn the wig a few times, you should wash it to make sure that the wig will last a long time.

① Let the Wig Soak

Fill a sink with warm water and wig shampoo. Put the wig in and let it sit for 10 minutes or so, then run your fingers through it as if you were washing your hair.

② Rinse

Pressing the wig gently to force water through it, rinse the whole thing 4 or 5 times. Add some conditioner to the water and rinse it again. If you add a little fabric softener when rinsing, it will help keep the wig from tangling.

③ Dry the Wig

Wrap the wig in a towel and gently press to squeeze out the excess water.

④ Let it Air Dry

Put the wig on a wig stand and let it naturally air dry. Once it has dried completely, spray it with wig spray and brush it well before storing it.

✿ Items for Wigs

The following items can be bought at wig stores, cosmetic shops, online, and at drugstores:

LIST	PRICE
Wig (heat-resistant, long, colored)	$30.00 to 100.00
Clip on Pigtails or Buns	$20.00 and up
Wig Net	$3.00 and up
Wig Stand (open type)	$5.00 to 10.00
Wig Stand (Styrofoam)	$10.00 to 20.00
Wig Brush	$8.00 to 10.00
Wig Spray	$6.00 to 10.00
Razor	$15.00 to 20.00
Wig Scissors	$12.00 and up
Hairspray	$5.00 to 10.00
Wig Shampoo	$5.00 to 15.00

Once the wig has been stored, it may get some wrinkles that are hard to get out. You might want to have a hat for returning from an event, or a separate wig for the ride home.

5−03 | Color Contacts

To match the eye color of your favorite character, you can use colored contacts. Contacts touch your eyes directly, so make sure you know how to use them properly.

How to Buy Color Contacts

Color contacts can easily be purchased on the internet. However, because they will sit directly on your eye, you may want to have an eye exam first, and ask your optometrist how to properly wear a contact, just to be safe. We recommend regular eye checkups.

Color contacts have a colored area that sits over your iris, allowing you to change the color of your eyes. They are sold as both prescription and nonprescription contacts.

How to Insert and Remove Color Contacts

Before touching your contacts, be sure to wash your hands. Also, make sure not to injure the lens or your eyes with your fingernails. Before putting the contacts in, insure that they are turned in the right way, with the lens on the outside. When the contacts are folded over, or turned inside out, use contact solution to reset the shape.

Outside

Inside

◆ How to Put Them In

Looking in the mirror, place the contact on your index finger, using your middle finger to hold open your lower eyelid.

Use your other hand's index finger to hold open your upper eyelid. Look straight ahead and place the lens directly over your iris.

Check that the color contact is sitting directly over your pupil, then slowly remove your finger. Blink many times to set the contact.

◆ How to Take Them Out

Stand before a mirror and look up with the eye you plan to remove the contact from.

Open your eye very wide and use your index finger to hold open your lower eyelid.

Using the thumb and index finger of your other hand, pinch the contact and it will come off the surface of your eyeball.

If you have never worn contacts before, be sure to practice a few times before the day of the event!

Warnings regarding color contact lenses:
- Make sure your hands are clean when handling contact lenses.
- Do not go to sleep with the contacts still in place.
- Do not share contact lenses with others.
- If the contacts feel strange on your eyes, see an optometrist.
- Read the instruction manual before using color contacts.

Your eyes may feel dry during an event, so try to apply eye drops every hour or so. Also, when it comes time to remove the contacts, make sure your fingertips are moist with contact solution, and they will come out smoothly. We also recommend that you wear the lenses for as short a time as possible.

Cleaning and Storing Your Contacts

After wearing contacts they must be washed and stored in contact cases. If storing the contacts is too much trouble, there are disposable contacts available, though they cost a little more.

①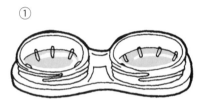

Wash the case and fill with contact solution.

②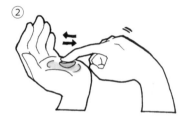

Cup your hand and fill it with contact solution. Place the contact in the puddle and swish it around with your fingertips for 10 seconds or so.

③

Hold the lens and apply contact solution to both sides.

④

Add the lenses to the contact case that has been filled with contact solution, and screw the caps down tightly. The contact solution should be changed out every week or so.

5-04 | Details

Once you have the makeup and wig and costume down, it's time to focus on the details. Here we go over some other fine points that you may want to consider.

Makeup other than Face-Makeup

We often think of makeup as something for our faces, but it is not strange at all to consider using makeup on other parts of our bodies that may be exposed. For example, our ears, arms, sides, and necks are often exposed and we forget to think of them as part of our costumes.

There is special foundation available for your body, but the same foundation that you use on your face should be just fine. Ensure that it is the same color as your skin, and use makeup wherever you feel like it!

Body Paint

There are many anime and manga characters that have characteristic markings on their arms and faces. To add these markings directly to your skin, we recommend body paint. There are products such as "face pens" that are sold for this purpose, and can be used just as easily as a pen can.

When you want to add a complicated design, or replicate a pattern perfectly, you can use temporary tattoos. You can scan the desired pattern and print it from your computer, then apply the pattern directly to your skin.

Pens are available for about $1.00 and temporary tattoo paper for around $10.00.

Nails

Nails that are too long or too dirty should be dealt with before the day of the event.

① Using a Nail File

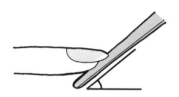

Hold the file at a 45 degree angle from the direction the nail grows.

② File from the Point

File in this order: point, sides, corners.

③ Smooth the Nails

Use a nail buffer to polish the surface of your nails. Use the buffer in order from rough to fine.

④ Finish

Apply a base coat to protect your nails, and you're done!

Depending on the character, you might paint them with a pattern, or even apply artificial nails. These can be found at a drugstore.

Removing Unwanted Hair

As you will be photographed at the event, even very fine details will show up in a good photograph. Be careful of the hair on your underarms, feet, legs, face, fingers, and your nose hairs. If you are wearing something open-backed, you will want to touch up your back hair too.

✿ Stockings

Because some Cosplay events have rules about exposed skin, it is typical to wear thick

stockings or tights when your costume requires your legs

to be exposed.

Business stockings are thin and transparent, and

therefore we recommend going with something thicker.

Choose the color based on your character. For example,

if you are a character from a fighting game, glossy

stockings may be appropriate.

If your costume requires your thighs to be exposed,

choose stockings that do not have elastic bands up

on the thighs (those vertical lines). Many sport tights or

dancer tights do not have these lines, and therefore are

great for Cosplaying. Gymnastic tights are stretchable,

durable, and thick, therefore we recommend them if you

can find them.

Clothing that exposes the upper thigh

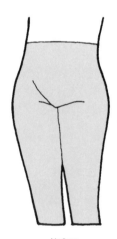

No lines   Elastic lines

❁ Underwear

Underwear that sits tight on the skin can show up as underwear lines under your costume. Even if you would not typically wear a G-string, they will not show under your costume, and therefore are great for Cosplaying. There is also some sport and gymnastic underwear that works well.

If the shoulders of your costume are open, you will want a bra with removable straps. If it makes you uncomfortable to wear a strapless bra, consider transparent straps. If your costume requires you to show a lot of chest, there are "nude bras" that work. In the very rare event that your nude bra slips, you may want to have a seal or sticker in place to cover your nipples. This will help set your mind at ease.

❁ Exposure

At Cosplay shows, there are times when people wear hot pants or spats under their shorts. This is because of the rare event that they may be secretly photographed.

Especially if the shorts are an integral part of the character design, and you want to make sure they are represented appropriately, we recommend that you wear additional shorts underneath. Also, you should avoid poses that might intentionally show off that area of your costume.

A way to avoid unintentional exposure is to wear "full body tights" which cover your whole body from toes up to your chest. These are great if your costume has high leg-slits or a very short skirt or hot pants.

Even if you feel like there is very little chance of exposing yourself in your costume, consider taking these preventative measures just in case.

Hiding Your Breasts

When women want to Cosplay as male characters, they often must hide their breasts. Here are some great items to help you do just that.

◆ Compression Shirts

These are something like a corset, though stretchy. They can be found for around $20.00 to $40.00, and are available online. They are probably the best way to hide your breasts. If the character calls for an exposed chest, tights can be worn over the compression shirt for a more natural look.

◆ Tape

Use tape over a tank top to press down and hide your breasts. It is cheap and easy to find, but it can slip if applied directly to skin and may interfere with your breathing.

◆ Kimono Bra

These can be bought at kimono supply shops in Japan. They are available for around $20.00 and are not so tight that they become uncomfortable after a long time. However, they are not suited to costumes that expose much of the chest. And they are only available in Japan.

That reminds me, there are items out there to make your breasts bigger, rather than hide them! There are more items than just wigs or contacts out there that will help bring your character to life!

Chapter 6

Participating in an Event

❶ Deciding on an Event

❷ What to Bring to the Event

❸ What Happens at the Event

❹ What to Watch Out for at Events

COLUMN Extra Advice

This chapter will go over all you need to know about Cosplay events. What makes an event easy to participate in, how do events normally progress, and what should you watch out for.

140

DID YOU GET BREAKFAST?

THE EVENTS ARE BUSY, AND WE MIGHT NOT HAVE TIME FOR LUNCH.

I DON'T EAT LUNCH, BUT ARE YOU GOING TO BE OKAY?

YUP!

TADA!

ENE in CHARGE

I BROUGHT A QUICK SNACK.

黄色い線

PLEASE STEP BEHIND THE YELLOW LINE

列車の側

夕闇 TOKYO, SHINAGAWA. TRAIN IS APPROACHING.

おお GUESS WE ARE ALL READY!

I WONDER IF I FORGOT ANYTHING.

I BROUGHT ALL MY STUFF. IF YOU NEED SOMETHING, JUST ASK!

RATTLE

RATTLE

SHOOO

THANKS!

RATTLE

RATTLE

SWISH

I WAS LOOKING ONLINE,

AND THERE ARE TONS OF COSPLAY EVENTS, ALL OVER THE PLACE!

THE COSPLAY CARNIVAL WE ARE GOING TO TODAY IS JUST ABOUT COSPLAY,

BUT THERE ARE COSPLAYING SECTIONS AT THE MARCH COMIC EVENT GOING ON NEXT WEEK, AND OFTEN AT FAN FOCUSED EVENTS!

I'VE NEVER BEEN TO A GENRE EVENT BEFORE, BUT DO ALL THE COSPLAYERS AGREE TO FOCUS ON A PARTICULAR THEME?

YES!

PEOPLE WITH THE SAME TASTES ALL GET TOGETHER, SO IT'S EASY TO MAKE FRIENDS!

YOU CAN EVEN PICK THE EVENT BY THE CHARACTER YOU WANT TO BE!

WOW!

I WANT TO TRY ALL KINDS OF THINGS!

143

UM, UM...

A NORMAL GUEST OR A COSPLAYER?

I, UH...

THERE'S THE ENTRANCE!

WE JUST PAY ON OUR WAY IN, RIGHT?

THIS EVENT EVEN CHARGES A DIFFERENT TICKET PRICE DEPENDING ON WHETHER OR NOT YOU ARE COSPLAYING.

THEY DO?

I'M A COSPLAYER!

THAT'LL BE 1,500 YEN PLEASE.

OVER THERE!

YUP

WOMEN'S CHANGING ROOM

女性更衣室 →

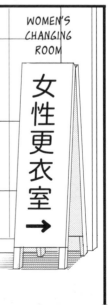

SEE THOSE LINES ON THE FLOOR?

THIS CREATES A SPACE FOR ONE PERSON. YOU HAVE TO CHANGE WITHIN YOUR OWN SPACE.

THEY SURE DO HAVE A LOT OF RULES...

EVEN IF THERE AREN'T LINES, KEEP IN MIND THAT PEOPLE ARE COMING IN BEHIND YOU, SO TRY TO MOVE AS FAR BACK AS YOU CAN.

TO THE BACK!
後ろのほうへ
行こう!

OKAY.

AND DON'T DO ANYTHING THAT WOULD BOTHER ANYONE ELSE, LIKE USING AEROSOL SPRAYS OR TAKING A BUNCH OF PICTURES.

CHEESE!
ハイチーズ!

着替え

BUT I'M CHANGING...

SPRAY

OKAY.
うん

JUST TRY TO MAKE SURE YOU KEEP YOUR THINGS IN YOUR OWN SPACE. YOU DON'T WANT TO BE IN SOMEONE ELSE'S SPACE.

CLACK

PEOPLE JUST KEEP ON COMING IN BEHIND US.

I HAVE TO CHANGE IN SUCH A SMALL SPACE.

I'LL JUST GET MY BOOTS FOR NOW.

CLACK

CLIP

FWOOSH

IT'S A LITTLE OFF

DUDUM!

RIKO, YOU'RE SO FAST!

*SOME EVENTS HAVE SEPARATE CHANGING AND MAKE-UP SPACES.

I BETTER SPEED IT UP!

RUFFLE

RUFFLE

Chapter

6-01 | Deciding on an Event

There are many different kinds of events that you can Cosplay at.
Depending on the type of event, the rules, and where it is being held,
you can have your pick of what event you want to go to!

✿ Types of Events

◆ Cosplay Events

These are events where the main goal is Cosplaying. There are Cosplayers and photographers

in attendance. There are often places for photography set up and some props may be available.

Sometimes the events are held outside, or at a park, or at an amusement park.

◆ Events at Which You Can Cosplay

These events are not set up specifically for Cosplaying, but they welcome Cosplay participation.

Comic conventions are this type. They may only allow Cosplay photography in a designated

area, or may only allow shopkeepers to Cosplay.

What Makes an Event Easy to Participate In?

There are two things that make an event easy to participate in: 1) ease of access 2) how comfortable an environment that has been set up.

◆ Ease of Access:

The ease of access is simple to look into before hand.

Participating in a Cosplay event involves transporting a fair amount of luggage. If you are going by train, make sure you see how close the nearest station is to the event hall. If there is a bus, how often does it run? Are there taxis available? If it is a large event, they may be running more busses than normal.

◆ How Comfortable is the Environment:

It might be difficult to judge how comfortable the environment is at first, but look into things like: Do they have a system for storing luggage? Are there changing rooms with enough space? Is there a designated photography area? Look at the website and read people's comments. If the

event is held outside, will there be a pavilion in case of bad weather. This last point is very important!

Things to Keep in Mind When Deciding on an Event

When it comes down to choosing an event, don't think about what kind of event you want to go to, think about why you want to go to an event. Focusing on your motivation will make it clear what event is for you.

◆ "I want to just try out Cosplay and see if I like it."

→ Local Events

If you don't have a particular goal in mind, but just want to try it out and are nervous, start with a local event. Instead of going somewhere you don't know, staying close to home will make it less scary, and transport will be that much simpler.

◆ "I want to meet and hang out with people who like the same manga or anime."

→ Genre Events

If there is a particular show or manga that you like and you have a character that you like, why not go to an event that focuses on that series, for fans of that series. These are fun because it tends to be easy to meet people.

◆ "I want more than just Cosplay. I want to have fun. And I want to dance."

→ Dance Party Events

At dance party events, the fun doesn't end with Cosplaying. Because these often involve moving your body a lot, not all costumes are suited for it, but if you like to move and exercise and have fun, these events are for you.

◆ **"I want to take nice pictures and have a nice relaxing time."**

→ Cosplay Photography Events

Cosplay photography events are held in rented out photography studios or event halls. They tend to be a little more expensive to participate in and are really for more intermediate level Cosplayers. They are slow moving and small, so it is nice to take your time and relax. Try to pick a place that matches the feeling of the series you are Cosplaying.

◆ **"I want to watch other people Cosplay."**

→ San Diego Comic Con and New York Comic Con

If it is your first time participating, it's best to avoid large events, but if you are just going to watch, then these are the best. People come from all over the country, giving you opportunities to meet and speak with all kinds of Cosplayers. You can see minor series and old series represented, and can see the most experienced Cosplayers around. When it comes time to participate, big events are fun because you get to show off your costume to large crowds of people.

Events Best Avoided by Beginners

Large events can take place in the summer and fall. They are packed with large crowds of people that do not Cosplay, and are so crowded that everything takes a lot of time. They can be exhausting, and therefore are best avoided by beginners. Having said that, because people come from all over to participate in them, you are sure to meet a lot of interesting people that will recognize minor series.

Also, at large events like the San Diego Comic Con, they may have smaller events running strictly for Cosplaying at the same time as the main events are happening.

You have to bring your costume, props, makeup kit, and all sorts of other things to events. Here we introduce you to the essentials. Make sure not to forget anything!

✿ What to Bring

There are many things you will bring to the event. You may want to split them into two cases, one that you can keep with you for the whole time, and another that you can store at the counter during the event.

Make a list of the things you will need on the big day, and check it twice to make sure you don't forget anything.

Carry On	Check In
• Valuables • Camera • Small Tripod (some events do not allow tripods) • Business cards and business card holder • Small mirror • Cellular phone • Portable makeup kit (see chapter 5) • Face blotting paper • Snacks (for when there is no time to eat) • Eye drops for contacts • Copy of the manga your character is from (to look at poses) • Double sided tape (for quick fixes) • Safety Pins • Event Catalog (sometimes necessary as a ticket to the event)	• Makeup tools • Your costume • Your props • Your wig and its tools (wig net, wax, and brush) • Mirror • Hair pins • Tape • Sewing set • Color contacts • Tissue paper • Trash bag • Makeup remover • Moist towelettes • A hat or wig for the ride home

❁ How to Carry Your Costume

The easiest way to carry your costume and props is in a wheeled suitcase. The type you use when traveling should work just fine. If you decide to buy a new one just for the event, the soft-sided ones are lighter, but we recommend you get the kind with swiveling wheels. When it comes time to pack, you should put your heavier items, like your makeup kit, on the bottom, and your costume should go on the top. When you put the costume in, try and keep it fluffy so that it doesn't wrinkle. Your wig case should be collapsible, making transport more convenient.

It may seem obvious, but it's not always a good idea to wear your costume on the way to an event. Also, keep in mind that your suitcase can be an annoyance in very crowded areas. Keep it close to you when you are on the move. If your case has swiveling wheels, it makes it easier to keep the case close.

It's not always a good idea to wear your costume on the way to an event.

Make sure your suitcase does not get in the way of others. Drag it behind you or keep it close by your side. We recommend the kind with swiveling wheels.

How to Carry Your Props

If you have already styled your wig perfectly, set it on a wig stand and put it in a wig case. A wig case can be purchased for around $10.00 at a wig store. If you are going to put it in your suitcase, just put the whole box in. If not, rest it on top of the suitcase and secure it in place.

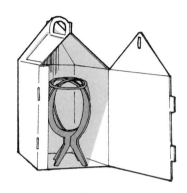

Wig Case

Weapons and large props should probably not go in your suitcase. Wrap them in fabric and put them in a bag that you will carry. The cloth will keep other people from seeing what is inside. Very large items should be made so they can be broken into parts and packed in boxes.

If your shoes are normal loafers or boots, just wear them to the event. Elevated boots are not made to be walked in for a long time, so they should probably be stored with your costume. There are also boot keepers designed for storing shoes, you can stuff one with newspaper to keep the shoes from wiggling around.

Business Cards

You will meet many Cosplayers and photographers at the event. It is therefore convenient to have a "business card" made for your Cosplay.

Normally they are designed on a computer. There are commercially available perforated card stocks for printing them, making the process simple.

Business cards can be printed on perforated card stock.

The companies that sell this card stock also have free software available for designing your cards. There is plenty of information available on their websites, so take a look!

Unfortunately, many of these papers do not print photographs very well. Once you get used to making your own cards, you can print photographs on different paper, then cut the cards out yourself.

Information to include on your cards includes the following: your picture, your Cosplay name, your website or blog address, and your contact information. If you include your personal information on the card, be careful who you hand it out to!

The best scenario is if you are in the costume you are wearing to the event, but it is not absolutely necessary. Consider having different cards for each of your costumes.

It does not matter if the card is horizontal or vertical.

Include whatever contact information you chose.

You might be nervous on the day of the event, to help you relax, let's go over the basic flow of the day.

✿ How to Prepare for the Big Day

If the tickets and catalogs are available for sale before the event begins, buy them in advance. The catalog will have the Cosplaying rules listed inside, be sure to read them. Make sure you know what is prohibited at the event.

Even if the catalogs are only available on the day of the event, the official website should have the rules listed in advance. Be sure to read them.

You will want to finish most of your packing a day or two in advance. Your costume, however, will wrinkle if you pack it in advance, so save it until the day of the event before putting it into your suitcase.

Typically the events run from the morning until around dusk. Depending on the time and location, you may have trouble finding a place to eat lunch, so make sure you eat a big breakfast. Some Cosplayers don't eat lunch because it interferes with their makeup, but there is no need to starve. Bring along some snacks for when you get hungry.

If you wear a wig during the event, you may have a hard time fixing your hair afterwards. So bring a hat or wig to wear on the way home. Your second wig should be a simple, natural style for the return ride.

❁ When You Arrive

Before leaving the house, make sure you know how to get to the event.

There may be a line of people waiting to get in. Calmly go to the back of the line and wait.

Cutting in line is strictly forbidden.

If the catalog and tickets are sold on the day of the event, they will be for sale at the entrance.

For Cosplay only events, the cost of a ticket will be different for Cosplayers and photographers. If you are asked how you will be participating, answer "as a Cosplayer."

After buying the catalog and ticket and reading through the rules, make your way to the changing rooms. Areas for makeup are different depending on the event, and they may be separate from the changing rooms. Look through the catalog, and if you don't understand where to go, ask a staff member.

❁ Changing Into Your Costume

There will be times when the space for one person is marked off, and times when it is not. If the space is set aside, make sure that you stay within it. If your costume is large and you absolutely need more space, talk to a staff member about using two adjacent spaces. If there are no designated spaces, just go to the back and use as little space as possible to change.

If you open your suitcase all the way, it will take up too much space, so only pry open the lid enough to get out what you need.

When you take off your clothes, put them where the costume used to be in your suitcase.

What to Watch Out for in the Changing Room

There will be rules for the event that dictate how you are to behave in the changing room.

First of all, you cannot take pictures in the changing room. Even if you are just taking pictures of you and your friends, someone changing in the background might end up in your picture, and they might accuse you of voyeurism. Some events may not want you using your cellphone either.

Most events prohibit the use of hairspray. When you are applying makeup, make sure it doesn't drip or get the room dirty.

When you are finished changing, leave the room quickly. There will be a meeting area outside of the chaining room. Bring any trash you have with you.

Events may not want you using the power outlets, so make sure your phone and other devices are fully charged before arriving.

Some events will have a counter with someone to hold your baggage during the event. It is convenient to drop off your suitcase after changing, but make sure you do not have any valuables stored in it.

No Photography

No Hairspray

Don't Make a Mess

Meet People Outside of the Changing Room

Don't Use the Power Outlets

Bring Your Trash With You

Going to the Photography Area

The photography area is a place to have fun, be with friends and take pictures of your costumes.

When you want to stand around and chat with friends, you should avoid hallways and photograph areas, as you might end up in the way of other people.

When it comes time to take pictures, photographers may line up to take a

picture of you. Depending on the event, some Cosplayers end up completely surrounded by photographers. If a crowd forms, indicate to the photographers the amount of time you will stand there, count down, and then ask them to disperse.

What to Watch out for When Taking Pictures

Taking pictures is probably the main attraction at Cosplay events, but it can also be fun to take, and have your picture taken, by friends.

When you are the one being photographed, keep the following things in mind:

◆ Being Photographed

When you are being photographed, keep your luggage behind you or off to the side so that it doesn't interfere with the photograph.

When the photographer leaves the pose up to you, try and pick a pose that your character often takes. We look more into poses in chapter 7.

When the photographer requests certain poses, know that you do not have to do anything that you are not comfortable with. Other than poses, if the angle, or the amount of time they are spending makes you uncomfortable, refuse to allow them to photograph you. There may be people that try to intentionally touch you. Tell them in a clear and unambiguous way that you do not want them to continue. If you feel nervous at anytime, speak to a staff member.

After the photography session has concluded, thank the photographer. They may give you a business card. If they do, give them your prepared cards as well.

◆ **Photographing Others**

When you find someone you would like to photograph, always ask for permission before you start taking pictures. If they refuse, absolutely do not photograph them.

If there is a line, make sure you enter from the back. When your turn comes up, thank the Cosplayer before photographing them.

If you would like them to take a particular pose, discuss it with them and agree on something. You must be specific. Also, even if you are the same gender, do not touch their body to show them how you would like them to stand.

If you would like to try a few poses, ask them to try out a few different poses. Keep in mind that others may be waiting, so do not spend too much time photographing someone, keep it to under 5 minutes and aim for 5 - 10 pictures. You should not take more than 30 pictures.

When you finish, thank the Cosplayer and give them your business card. This may lead to extended conversation, which is fine, but if there are other people waiting to take pictures then try to keep the conversation as short as possible. If you exchange business cards then you may have a chance of meeting them outside of the event as well.

6–04 | What to Watch Out for at Events

Chapter

Cosplay events are something everyone works on together. There are manners and rules that you should adhere to when participating.

 ## Events Belong to Everyone

Make sure to read the rules listed in the catalog so that you do not unintentionally bother other people. Basic manners are applicable: do to others what you would want done unto yourself. The event is not all about you. It is for everyone to enjoy.

◆ **Unlisted Rules:**

Even if they are not listed in the rules, there are still certain things you will want to keep in mind when attending an event.

- Cosplaying is not the same as completely becoming a character. There is nothing wrong with joking around with friends, but if behaving in the way your character behaves makes people uncomfortable, you should stop.
- Don't act in a way that degrades your character. If your character is very young, don't act sexual for example.
- Events are fun, and exciting places to be, but if you find yourself running around and screaming and hugging everyone, you might want to put the breaks on.
- When your weapons can do damage (sticks, bats, rackets) don't swing them around aimlessly.
- Do not be rude to the staff. They are working hard to make the event fun, so respect them and do as they ask.
- Don't overdo it. When you feel tired or sick, take a break.

No Secret Pictures!

It is a real shame, but there are some shady characters out there that target Cosplayers. They try to sneak pictures of you out in the event hall, and also sometimes in changing rooms. Be ready to deal with these unsavory types. Keep an eye out for the following:

- Whatever your costume calls for, always wear underwear. So even if you are in a swimsuit, wear a nude bra and a G-string underneath it.
- If your costume exposes a lot of skin, wear long stockings and full body stockings.
- Make your costume so that your underwear is not visible.
- Practice your poses in front of a mirror, and take note of angles that creeps might try to photograph you from.
- Luggage left in the changing rooms may contain a small hidden camera. If you find any strange luggage, report it to the staff immediately.
- In the unlikely event that someone has taken pictures of you without permission, confronting them directly may bring more trouble your way. Tell the staff immediately and let them deal with it.

Don't allow photography without permission!

Extra Advice

We have set up a little FAQ here regarding some doubts you may harbor towards events.

Q: Can I wear glasses while Cosplaying?

A: Of course you can, though if your character doesn't wear glasses, you may want to remove them for photographs.

Q: What do you not want other Cosplayers and photographers to do?

A: When people ask for obviously vulgar poses, or take a very long time photographing, they will draw the ire of others. If they continue what they are doing after being asked to stop, they will also be bothering others. Also, not only photographers, but Cosplayers as well, should not run around screaming in high voices and causing a ruckus. People will not like you if you do these things.

Q: What kind of camera should I buy?

A: At first, a simple digital compact will be just fine. If you can, chose one with a manual mode so that you can adjust shutter speed, ISO, and the F-stop.

Q: What is the best time to arrive at a Cosplay event?

A: All events are different, so there is no "right" answer, but large events like Comic Con may require you to line up for a while before being let in. Just as an estimate, why not try arriving an hour or thirty minutes before the start time?

What to do at the event, what to watch out for, what to bring… There are so many questions that a beginner might have! I want to look into all of these things so that I can enjoy my Cosplay life with as many other people as I can!

Chapter 7

Taking Beautiful Pictures

❶ How to Have Nice Pictures Taken

❷ The Basics of Cosplay Posing

❸ Retouching Photos

❹ Exhibiting Your Photos

COLUMN Facial Expressions

There are a lot of little things to consider for the best possible picture. Lighting and poses are just the beginning. In this chapter we will also go over easy ways to retouch and exhibit your photographs.

FIRST OF ALL...

RUSTLE

LET ME GET A SHOT OF YOU AT YOUR VERY FIRST COSPLAY EVENT!

WHAT? ME?

私!?

THUMP

CLICK!

I, UH... I...

もじ...

UM... PEACE!

とりあえず
ピース♪

CLICK!

NICE! THAT COSTUME LOOKS GREAT ON YOU!

SMILE

OH...
H'AHA

FOR THE NEXT ONE, LET'S HAVE YOU ACT A BIT MORE LIKE LUNCASIS!

MORE LIKE LUNCASIS?

BEEP
BEEP

168

WOW!

WOW RIKO, YOU'RE A GREAT PHOTOGRAPHER!

NAH...

YOU CAN MAKE THEM LOOK EVEN BETTER BY ADJUSTING THEM ON A COMPUTER!

ADJUST PICTURES?

YOU CAN ADJUST THINGS LIKE BRIGHTNESS,

AND EVEN SAVE PICTURES THAT YOU THOUGHT WERE NO GOOD!

before   after

NEAT!

HOW CONVENIENT!

YOU CAN EVEN ERASE THINGS YOU DON'T WANT THERE, LIKE PIMPLES OR MOLES. YOU CAN CHANGE THE COLOR OF YOUR EYES AND BLUR THE BACKGROUND TOO!

— EYE COLOR
目の色

— PIMPLES
ニキビ跡

— BACKGROUND
光景

— MOLES
ホクロ

WOW!

171

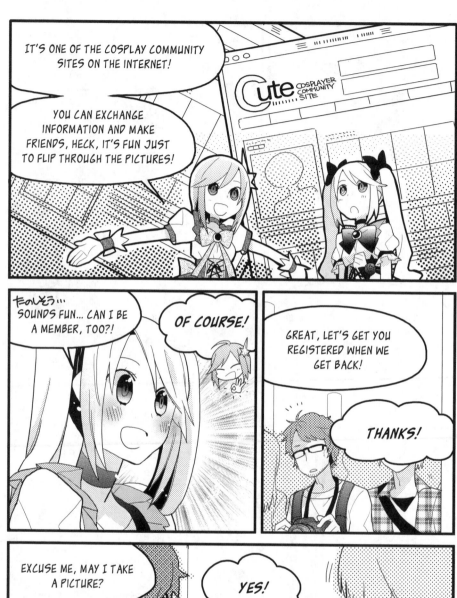

IT'S ONE OF THE COSPLAY COMMUNITY SITES ON THE INTERNET!

YOU CAN EXCHANGE INFORMATION AND MAKE FRIENDS, HECK, IT'S FUN JUST TO FLIP THROUGH THE PICTURES!

Cute COSPLAYER COMMUNITY SITE

SOUNDS FUN... CAN I BE A MEMBER, TOO?!

OF COURSE!

GREAT, LET'S GET YOU REGISTERED WHEN WE GET BACK!

THANKS!

EXCUSE ME, MAY I TAKE A PICTURE?

YES!

THUMP

THUMP

173

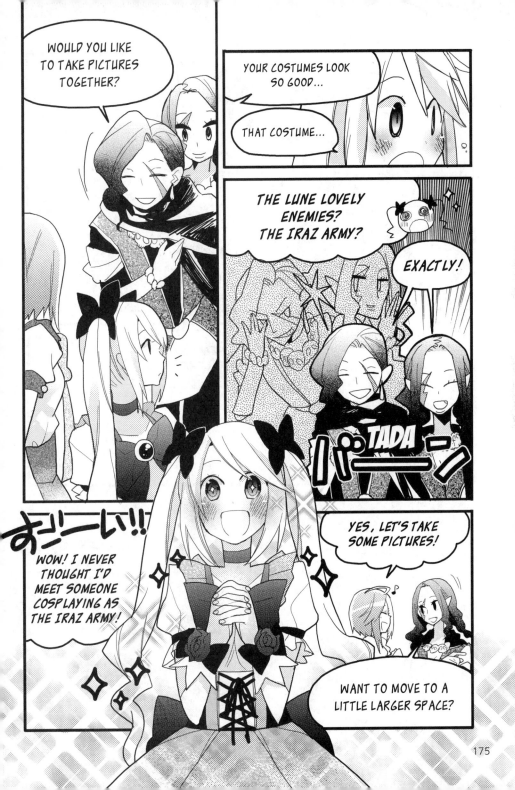

HOW SHOULD WE POSE?

THERE ARE PEOPLE LINING UP!

THE QUALITY IS AMAZING! LUNE LOVELY AND IRAZ!

ルンリ イラ！

オリ゛ティすげ゛え

LEMME GET MY CAMERA READY. 撮ろうかね〜

COSPLAY EVENTS SURE ARE...

10からとりまーす

10

9...

I'LL COUNT DOWN!

FUN!

CLICK!

7-01 | How to Have Nice Pictures Taken

Poses and expressions have a big impact on the final picture. Practice your poses before you head to the event and figure out what looks the best.

Good Places for Photography

It is nice if there is no space for people to walk behind you and mess up the background, for example, against a wall is good. But don't use a space for too long. Let other people have a chance.

About Lighting

You should always be aware of the direction the light is coming from. If the light is coming from straight ahead, it might make your face shine too much and you will be squinting in the picture. On the other hand, backlighting will cast your face in shadow, while unnecessary light will come into the lens at an angle, resulting in a photograph that is too bright.

We recommend side lighting, with the light coming behind you at a diagonal angle. Your outline will be sharp and the picture will turn out best with this lighting. If you have to be backlit, even altering the angle by a few degrees can make a big difference.

Backlit

Backlit at an Angle

7-02 | The Basics of Cosplay Posing

Your pose and facial expression will have a big impact on the final photograph. Practice your poses before you head to the event and figure out what looks the best.

 ## Points to Remember

The most important thing to keep in mind is the attitude of your character. In other words, you should pick your pose from actual poses the character makes in the work they are a part of. The following specific scenes are a great place to start pose hunting.

- **The character's first appearance**
- **Famous scenes**
- **Book and movie packages**
- **Official character guides**

- **The character's finishing moves**
- **Commercial scenes**
- **Posters and cards**
- **Figurines**

Also look through some online community sites to get an idea of the types of poses people use.

 ## Think About How You Stand

Just standing and facing the camera results in a photograph with no sense of movement, a boring photograph. If you stand diagonally with your torso turned, you will look better in the picture. If you put your right foot forward, drop your left foot back, you will also look more dynamic. If you put your left arm forward, drop your right arm back, and so on, it can help spice up the pose a lot. If you keep these things in mind you will naturally turn diagonally toward the camera.

Diagonal Pose

✿ Think About Your Hands

By using your hands, you can add a lot of variety to your poses.

Put your hand toward the camera, put it up by your collarbone, run it through your hair, or touch your necklace. These things can help. Even just crossing your arms or touching your chin will add a sense of movement to the photo.

Hand Toward the Camera

Hands Near Collarbone   Hands Running Through Your Hair   Hands Touching Your Hair

✿ Use Your Costume

We think poses that use your costume look great. Grabbing your skirt, putting your hands in your pockets, throwing a jacket over your shoulder, etc. If there is something noteworthy on your back, turn around and look over your shoulder.

Sitting Down Poses

You can put your legs out before you, cross them,

sit cross-legged, or put your legs out to the side.

If you are just going to sit there, put your props

around you to add some spice.

If you are in a short skirt or dress, take care to not

accidentally expose yourself.

If your character is a woman, placing your hands

on your knees will give a sense of elegance to the

pose.

This pose is an example of sitting with your legs to the side and hands on your lap.

Use Your Props

Using props in your poses is an accepted norm.

Use those swords, guns, sticks, and student bags

you made!

If you are going to use props for your pose, consult

the manga, or posters for the characters famous

finishing moves or poses. If a character's weapon is

particularly famous, hold it over your back and look

over your shoulder to display it.

Props will also help you to do a casual, normal

pose. A ring of flowers or a little stuffed animal

can make a big difference. If you are nervous or

Characters with famous weapons can be held over your back for a dynamic photo.

too embarrassed to really let yourself go with the character's poses, we recommend using the

character's props to give a sense of place and feeling to the character. It is much better than

simply standing there.

You might be nervous or hesitant the first time you pose before a camera, but pretend you are a

model and let yourself go!

❊ The Difference Between Girl and Boy Poses

As we explained in a previous section, the placement of your hands and feet can change the way your character appears. Keep the gender of your character in mind!

◆ How to Stand

Standing with your feet facing outwards is fine, but if you stand with your feet facing inwards, it will lend a girlish, cute overall impression to the photograph. Boy characters would stand with their feet at the width of their shoulders and with their feet facing out.

Women stand with feet pointed inwards.

Men stand with legs apart and feet pointed outwards.

◆ How to Make a Fist

It may seem a little subtle, but the shape of your fist can also have an impact on the gender of your character. The fist on the left is for women, while the fist on the right is for men.

For a feminine fist, the thumb is on the outside, and the fingers are loose. The wrist is slightly bent outwards.

For a masculine wrist, the thumb is bent inwards, and the fingers a curled tightly. The wrist is bent slightly inwards.

Your wrists can affect your pose in the following way.

For characters from fighting games, use a masculine wrist.

🌸 Pair Poses

◆ When a Masculine Character Takes a Feminine Character's Hand

When a man reaches for a woman's hand, the woman responds by placing her hand on top of the man's.

◆ Standing Together

If you both hug from the front, or too tightly, your costumes won't end up showing much in the picture.

Put your weight into your hips, with the hips close together and lean away from each other a little.

When you look into each other's eyes turn so that you are both slightly diagonal to the camera.

7-03 | Retouching Photos

By using computer software, you can easily retouch your photographs to make them look better.

 ## Retouching Basics

In this section we will go over simple and effective tools for fixing your photographs. Brightness and color balance (white balance, skin cleanup, and eye color alteration).

◆ What You Can Do with Software.

Photo retouching involves using simple software to adjust the values of your photographs. You can erase moles and pimples, wrinkles, and even change the color of your eyes. You can add highlights and shadows to improve the look of a photograph.

◆ Photo Retouching Software

The most well known photography editing software is Adobe's Photoshop. But for beginners, Photoshop Elements should be sufficient. It is much cheaper than the full version of Photoshop, and has enough features.

For the remainder of this chapter, all examples will be given for Photoshop Elements.

◆ Things to Learn Beforehand

• Save the original file.

Before you start altering a photograph, make sure you have saved a copy of the original. You can do this with layers, or just make a copy of the actual file on your hard drive. This is so you can revert to the original in case you make a mistake.

When you make a mistake:

Click on edit from the toolbar and select "Undo."

 ## Adjusting the Brightness

To adjust the overall brightness and effect of an image, use the color adjustment feature and the contrast feature. These selections will allow you to change the values for your picture. They are very convenient.

If you want to adjust these values on your own, open the brightness and contrast menus.

Once you open Brightness/Contrast, a dialog box will appear with two sliders, one for brightness and one for contrast. Slide the buttons to adjust the values to your desired effect.

 ## Erasing Moles and Pimples

To erase unwanted blemishes, use the copy stamp tool. Open the tool menu and choose the copy stamp tool. Press the ALT key and click on a nice area of your skin. This selects the area you will be copying FROM. Release the ALT key and the cursor will return. Click on the blemish you want to remove and the program will copy from the area you already selected to cover it.

✿ Skin Cleanup

When you want to make your skin look better, choose the blur tool from the tool menu. Click on the area you want to blur and move the cursor in slow circles. It will slowly blur over blemishes and rough spots. Play around with the size and harshness of the brush tool for different results.

✿ Change Your Eye Color

If you cannot wear color contacts, or forgot them when it was time for pictures, you can change the color of your eyes with computer software.

1. Create a layer for color contacts. From the layer menu, choose "New Layer."

2. Use the magnifier tool to zoom in on your eyes, then reverse foreground and background color.

3. A color picker will open, chose the color you want to make your eyes and click OK.

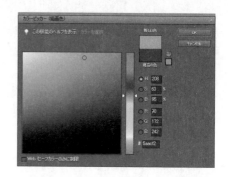

4. Use the brush to paint the desired color over your eyes. We will make it look natural later, so for now, just cover the area with the desired color.

5. Change the layer mode from Normal to Screen. Changing the mode will make your eyes look more natural.

6. Now your photograph will look as though you had color contacts in.

Register with a Cosplay Community Site

After the event, you might want to continue the fun on a community site.

If you have accounts at many different sites, there is nothing wrong with uploading the same

content to them all.

Start a Blog or Website

You could also start your own blog to show off your pictures. You can then add the address to

your business cards or register the site with a Cosplay search engine.

What to Watch out for on the Internet

When you are exchanging photographs on the internet, be very careful with your personal

information. Your phone number, address, real name, occupation, workplace, and school name

are all personal information, and you should be very careful with who you give them to. You

should expect the people you are speaking with to behave in the same way. Do not expect

people to give out their personal information.

Facial Expressions

To take great pictures, your facial expression is just as important as your pose. If you don't feel like you can make a natural face in from of a camera, or you aren't sure how to smile, we have some advice!

Think About Your Character

Your expression should be a reflection of your character, just like your pose. Think about what the character would do, and try and bring that expression to life.

Get Used to Cameras

You must be relaxed to look good in pictures. Before you get used to it, you might feel nervous in front of a camera. To prevent this, try and get used to cameras in your daily life.

Understand Your Own Face

Human faces are not perfectly symmetrical. To make cute faces and expand your "expression repertoire," train your facial muscles. A quick search on the web will turn up many ways to do this.

Normally pictures are taken by looking straight into the lens, but if you feel like it helps express your character, you can try looking off in a different direction. Looking slowly up from a low position, like a fox, gives some dynamic movement to the picture and looks great! The more you practice your expressions, the more characters you'll be able to bring to life!

Epilogue

THAT WAS SO MUCH FUN!

I THOUGHT COSPLAY WAS SOMETHING REALLY HARD!

ALL OF IT THANKS TO YOU, RIKO!

BUT IT WAS SO MUCH FUN, MAKING THE COSTUME AND MAKING FRIENDS!

THANKS A LOT.

THAT'S NOT TRUE, YOU MADE THAT WHOLE COSTUME ON YOUR OWN, REIA! THAT LOOKS AMAZING,

ESPECIALLY FOR YOUR FIRST TIME!

NO, THANK YOU! I'M GLAD WE GOT TO BE LUNE LOVELY TOGETHER!

SO THAT WAS MY COSPLAY DEBUT...

YUP, AND YOU DID A GREAT JOB!

ほんねSIGH

THAT REMINDS ME... I...

RUSTLE RUSTLE

I REALLY WANTED TO GIVE YOU THIS BEFORE THE EVENT...

I HOPE YOU LIKE IT.

HUH? FOR ME?

OOHHH

OOHHH

WHAT COULD IT BE?

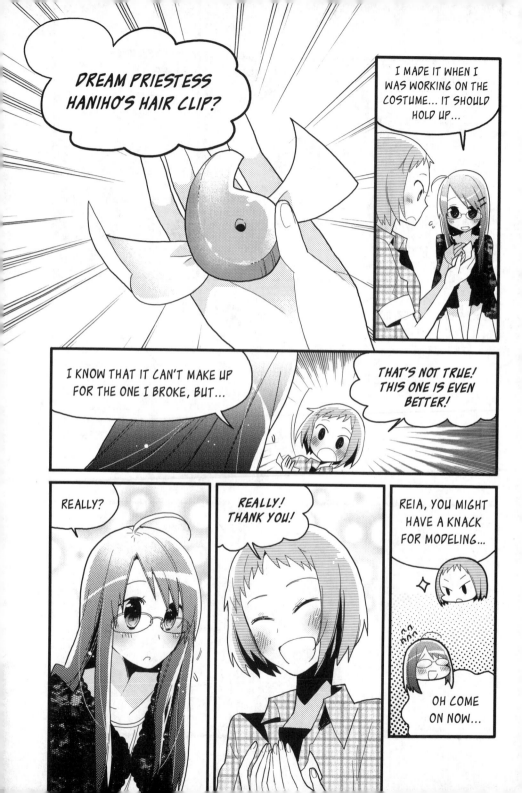

Afterword

This book, just as the title suggests, was written with the Cosplay beginner in mind.

We thought about a person who wants to try Cosplay, but doesn't know where to start. We went through all of our own experiences, where we messed up, what we learned from, and what made us happy. We hope to have given good suggestions to the true beginner.

The idea of dressing up as imaginary characters may seem strange at first glance. You may want to try it, but feel embarrassed. But that desire to try is the first step into the Cosplaying world. You do not need a great amount of talent of skill to try Cosplay. You do not need to change your lifestyle or hobbies. All you need to do is add Cosplay to the list of things you would like to try.

All the information we have collected in this book represents only a small portion of what you can do with Cosplay. There are no absolute rules in Cosplay. Feel free to look through the book and find what you like. Find your own way to Cosplay!

"I want to look like my favorite character!"
"I want to try and make that costume!"
"I want to take neat pictures!"
"I want to meet people who share my interests!"

There are many reasons why people start Cosplaying. Just like the characters in the manga sections of this book, we hope this book will help many people take that first step into Cosplay.

November 2011

Takasou & RUMINE

Bios

Yuki Takasou is an avid cosplayer and costume designer. She spends her time offering help and advice to other fellow cosplayers, such as creating free costume patterns. She also actively helps support the cosplay online community by offering help to dedicated start-up cosplay websites.

RUMINE is writer, designer and teacher. She is an aspiring actor and voice actor. She enjoys and supports the cosplay community and regularly receives new orders for her original costume designs.